ASSAYS

VOLUME I

ASSAYS

CRITICAL APPROACHES
TO MEDIEVAL AND
RENAISSANCE TEXTS

Peggy A. Knapp and Michael A. Stugrin
Editors

UNIVERSITY OF PITTSBURGH PRESS

ASSAYS

Critical Approaches to Medieval and Renaissance Texts

is an annual edited by Peggy A. Knapp and Michael A. Stugrin and published by the University of Pittsburgh Press. The editors are seeking manuscripts which (1) make use of modern critical thought (structuralism, Marxism, psychoanalysis, feminism, and many other kinds) in order to illuminate medieval and Renaissance works (including Milton); (2) argue either for or against the usefulness of one or more contemporary critical stances for clarifying premodern works; (3) review the contribution of a particular theory to our understanding of early works; and (4) present the case for older critical methods or outline their relationship to more recent developments. Our object is to create an impartial, scholarly forum for debate about the connections between critical theory and early texts.

Please send articles to: The Editors, *Assays*, Department of English, Carnegie-Mellon University, Pittsburgh, Pa. 15213. Manuscripts should be prepared according to the MLA Style Sheet. Send a separate cover letter and return postage together with two copies of each submission. The article itself should not contain or imply the author's name or institutional affiliation, but should begin with the exact title mentioned in the cover letter. The editors are interested in insuring fairness and courtesy to all contributors.

Within the United States, *Assays* may be ordered from the University of Pittsburgh Press, Pittsburgh, Pa. 15260.

Overseas orders should be addressed to Feffer and Simons, Inc., 100 Park Avenue, New York, N.Y. 10017, U.S.A.

Published by the University of Pittsburgh Press, Pittsburgh, Pa. 15260
Copyright © 1981, University of Pittsburgh Press
All rights reserved
Feffer and Simons, Inc., London
Manufactured in the United States of America
Composition by the Publications Office, Carnegie-Mellon University

Library of Congress Catalog Card Number 80-54059
ISSN 0275-0058
ISBN 0-8229-3439-6

Contents

Editors' Preface

*T*he editors are proud to present this first volume in an annual series devoted to the interpretation of medieval and Renaissance materials. Our hope is that the current explosion of interest in and controversy over the nature of the interpretive task (including developments in semiotics, linguistics, philosophy of language, and Marxist and Freudian theory) will help us all to rethink our understanding of our legacy of art and thought from these early periods. It should also impel us to refine established methods for inquiry and discover new ones. *Assays* aspires to be a forum for such investigations and for the new readings of old texts which will result.

We think this volume exemplifies the goals toward which *Assays* is striving. We are not the organ of any particular philosophy of interpretation or the champion only of what is new-born. Some of the essays presented here *do* arise directly from concerns recently voiced, in this country and in Europe, about the nature of writer, audience, and language. Others are rooted in the more familiar terrains of intellectual history and patristic exegesis. They reflect each other because they all willingly join in a search for clarity in method and soundness in reading, in a shared sense of the metamorphosis of ideas across time, and in their emphasis on the complexity of their materials—whether philosophical treatises or imaginative literature.

We were saddened last year, like so many others who knew her, by the death of Elizabeth Salter of York University, England. She was a member of our original advisory board. Her scholarly breadth and personal enthusiasm would have contributed greatly to our enterprise.

Our debts in this inaugural volume are many. First we must thank our eminent and hard-working advisory board, who saw the need for such a venture as this one and believed in its feasibility. We also received advice from expert readers in various corners of the vast field of medieval and Renaissance studies. We are grateful to Jerome L.

Rosenberg, Dean of the Faculty of Arts and Sciences at the University of Pittsburgh, and J. Patrick Crecine, Dean of the College of Humanities and Social Sciences at Carnegie-Mellon University (CMU), for seed money to launch *Assays,* and to Frederick A. Hetzel, Director of the University of Pittsburgh Press, for taking us on. The production of our book is an experimental foray into computer editing and composing systems. In this, we have benefited from the knowledgeable and friendly work of Donna Walters and Tom Kosak (Publications Office, CMU), Catherine Marshall (University of Pittsburgh Press), John Stuckey (Director of Computing, Humanities and Social Sciences, CMU), and Charles Augustine (CMU Computation Center) in getting a handsomely printed volume together. From the very first, Andrew Ragan (CMU, class of 1981) has found out how to do magical things with computer text editing systems and then has done them. To him, and to Jennifer Donaldson (CMU, class of 1981), another able student assistant, much thanks.

Finally, we wish to invite readers to join this dialogue about interpretation.

ASSAYS

Cosmetic Theology:
The Transformation of a Stoic Theme

Marcia L. Colish

*T*he ethical significance of an individual's presentation of self is a topic that has inspired the interest of moralists since antiquity. It has fascinated Christian theologians no less than classical philosophers. During the period from the third century to the early fifth century this theme received the canonical form in which Christian thinkers bequeathed it to the Middle Ages and more recent times. The Latin apologists and church fathers who developed the range of positions on cosmetic theology which later became standard, drew on a number of sources for this purpose. Apart from the Bible and the conceptions of modesty derived from contemporary fashion and social convention, they also made use of philosophical treatments of the subject that had been in circulation since the days of the ancient Cynics. More recently, and more influentially, this classical tradition had been expressed by the Stoics and the Roman authors who drew upon them. The basic teaching of the Stoics on this point was that it is immoral to alter one's natural appearance. Classical Latin writers, whether they supported or satirized this principle, gave it a wide currency. The early Christian theologians reformulated the Stoic position in the light of scriptural counsels and ecclesiastical needs. In so doing they shifted decisively the original focus of the doctrine, applying cosmetic theology primarily to women. They therefore made it possible to connect this *topos* with the anti-feminist tradition which they inherited from the ancient schools of rhetoric. The transformation which Stoic cosmetic theology received in Christian hands thus involved more than the use of Stoic ethics for Christian ends; it also involved a more basic change in attitude toward the ethical character of the female sex as such.

Cosmetic theology was one of a number of ethical ideas that the ancient Stoics took over from the Cynics in the fourth century B.C. The Cynics had deliberately leveled a broadside against conventional

3

morality in all quarters, partly to *épater les bourgeois* and partly to raise questions about the intrinsic rationality of customary modes of behavior. The Cynics' position on the individual's presentation of self, as a feature of their argument for the moral equality of the sexes, sought to undermine the traditional distinctions between masculine and feminine activities deemed appropriate at the time. They applied this doctrine not only to a view of marriage that did away with the double standard of sexual ethics and replaced it with a relationship between equals, but also to the socialization and appearance of the sexes. Men and women, they argued, should wear the same kinds of clothing and receive the same education. The Cynics were moralists, essentially and exclusively. They did not try to provide a metaphysical or anthropological foundation for their ethical philosophy.[1] This was an omission that the ancient Stoics rectified. Their own ethics was based on a distinct theory of human nature which in turn was integrally related to their physics.[2]

For the Stoics, the human *logos* is a fragment of the divine *logos* which permeates and governs the natural universe. Consubstantial with God, the human mind functions in an analogous manner in ruling the human constitution. Just as reason and nature are identical on the cosmic level, so they are identical on a human level. They exercise the same normative role in individual and social morality. The Stoics thus define virtue as life in accordance with nature, or life in accordance with reason, which for them means the same thing. Outside of imparting a rigorously intellectualistic character to their conception of what is natural for man, this principle is central to Stoic ethics. Virtually all the school's moral teachings flow directly from it.

The two most important corollaries of the Stoic doctrine of *naturam sequere* for our immediate purposes are the moral equality of all human beings and the imitation of nature as a rule for ethical behavior. For the Stoics, all men are equal thanks to their common possession of the *logos*. On this basis the idea of sexual equality is given a solid philosophical foundation in Stoic thought.[3] Secondly, the Stoics believed that man's natural needs were few, and that they could be viewed primarily as intellectual rather than as physical needs. Not all members of the school were equally ascetic on this point. Some Stoics admitted physical needs as *adiaphora* or things indifferent. Classified as such, the *adiaphora* were grouped with the vicissitudes of life, graded as more or less preferable, and treated as not inconsistent with the pursuit of virtue although as distinct in kind and as detachable *en bloc* from the *summum bonum*. One of the chief indices of how rigorous or moderate an individual Stoic is on the doctrine of the preferables is his position on hair, which brings us to the topic of cosmetic theology as a feature of Stoic ethics.

The fact that matters tonsorial rather than matters cosmetic in the strict sense serve as the barometer underlines an important aspect of the Stoic treatment of this theme. Although the Stoics were vigorous defenders of the principle of sexual equality and although they do mention feminine beautifications to some extent in this context, their chief focus as cosmetic theologians is the personal style adopted by men and the effect that masculine modes of self-presentation have on other men. This point may be illustrated by a comparison among three of the Roman Stoics, Epictetus, Musonius Rufus, and Seneca. Musonius Rufus (A.D. 30-end of the first century) and his disciple Epictetus (ca. 50-130) are staunch representatives of the rigorist side of the Stoic school. They reflect this position by arguing that men should not cut their hair or shave their beards. If men were intended by nature to have short hair and smooth faces, nature would have provided them with these attributes. Since this is not the case, such tonsorial tamperings with nature should be shunned. Moreover, the departure from the usual Roman style which this practice entails will earmark the individual who adopts it as a sage, guided by nature and reason and not by convention.[4]

On the other hand, Seneca (4 B.C.-A.D. 65) takes a more moderate position.[5] He regards a man's unwillingness to resort to a barber as foolish, along with any other form of bizarre behavior. What is important, in ethical terms, is the inner intentionality that informs the outward act. As Seneca points out, with both wit and acuity, the slob may be just as much a poseur as the fop. An unconventional presentation of self may mask a perverted desire for self-display. In particular, Seneca argues, a man should follow the ordinary tonsorial rules. He should be clean-shaven, with neatly trimmed hair on his head and depilated armpits. However, he should avoid the depilation of his arms and legs and the removal of his pubic hair. The former practice is effeminate while the latter bespeaks the profession of the male homosexual prostitute. Seneca's reasons for these prescriptions, which may tell us more about the barbering of the first-century Roman male than we bargained for, have to do not only with the correspondence of a man's behavior with a correct ethical intention on a subjective level but also with the objective, or public relations, dimension. A sage, he explains, seeks to promote his philosophy by example as well as by precept. Deliberate bad grooming would be imprudent as a missionary tactic because it would alienate the audience that the philosopher wishes to attract.

The same kind of emphasis on the appearance of men and its pro-
paedeutic effect on other men informs the treatment of cosmetic
theology found in the Roman satirists. Not all of the satirists were
closely connected with the Stoa and, whether they were or not, they felt
free to supplement their presentation of this theme with rhetorical *topoi*.
There was, however, one Roman writer in this genre who was a Stoic
satirist par excellence. Persius (A.D. 34–62) was the disciple of the Stoic
teacher Cornutus, an associate of Seneca and his nephew Lucan, and
related by blood to members of the so-called Stoic opposition to Nero
which surfaced after Persius' death in the Pisonian conspiracy of A.D.
65. Persius himself remained aloof from political embroilments and
court intrigue. Despite his own personal predilections, he emphasizes
the obligation of the Stoic sage to serve his fellow man in his choice of a
career. The most pervasive ethical theme in his poems is the moral
imperative of public service. Persius aligns himself with the rigorist
branch of the Roman Stoa but he takes a position on hair that reflects
neither the ascetic nor the moderate view. He depicts the Stoic philosopher as a man with a shaven head.[6] While this idea is unique to Persius,
he follows a traditional line in his fourth satire. In this poem he casti-
gates a hypocritical and self-serving politician named Alcibiades, whose
depilation of his pubic hair is a metaphor for his selling of himself to the
crowd.[7] The connection with Stoic cosmetic theology is clear here
although Persius does not invoke the norms of nature or prudence in
either of these passages.

There is a distinct shift in tone in the satires of Juvenal (ca. 60–ca.
140). Although he sometimes refers to Stoicism as a philosophy whose
austere and upright morality is consistent with the *mos maiorem* now so
deplorably debased by the irresponsible aristocrats, the upstart mer-
chants, and the oriental corruptions of the day, he is by no means an
orthodox adherent of Stoic ethics. An excellent index of his departures
from that school is Juvenal's frontal attack on women in his sixth satire.
In this poem he criticizes women for some traits and tastes, such as
intelligence, scholarship, and the wearing of unisex clothing, which the
Stoics supported. The unadulterated misogyny expressed in the sixth
satire is derived rather from the *topoi* of antifeminist rhetoric. It deprives women, in Juvenal's view, of the potential for moral improve-
ment possessed by men; even if an exemplary woman of the old school
could be found, a veritable Cornelia, her very rigor and *gravitas* would
make her impossible to live with.[8]

While Juvenal's sixth satire provides a wealth of material for the
antifeminist orientation, it would be a mistake to limit his satirical
outlook to the female sex alone. The vast majority of Juvenal's satires

are directed against men, who, he states, are far more reprehensible as a group than women.[9] The range of activities in which custom permits them to engage multiplies their opportunities for wrongdoing. This is a theme which Juvenal orchestrates throughout his work. The most telling case in point is his second satire. In this poem, Juvenal's targets are frauds and perverts. They try to pass themselves off as philosophers, decorating their homes with busts and pictures of the ancient Stoics, such as Cleanthes and Chrysippus.[10] They also adopt tonsorial styles for those parts of their bodies, visible when they are clothed, which are associated with the Stoics,[11] although here Juvenal has to modify the trope of the bearded philosopher in the light of the fact that the fashion for beards initiated by the emperors in the second century had changed the status of this convention. In any event, the external appearance of the "Stoicidae"[12] or make-believe Stoics whom he berates, masks a vicious reality. These men wallow in the vices they denounce in others, especially lust, just as their clothing covers bodies whose strategic depilation is a witness of their moral degradation.[13] Like the misogyny of his sixth satire, Juvenal's hostility toward homosexuality, which he also attacks in his ninth satire, is remote from Stoic values. In both cases he sees the unacceptable behavior in question as a consequence of Rome's capitulation to insidious foreign customs. He repeatedly refers to these luxuries and depravities as the root cause of Rome's moral decay. While his treatment of cosmetic theology invokes the Stoic formulae in some respects, Juvenal thus situates it in a value system based on xenophobia and snobbery rather than in the Stoic context of virtue as life in accordance with nature.

A still more fundamental change is at hand as we move to the first and most influential treatment of cosmetic theology by a Christian author, Tertullian (ca. 155–220). Tertullian is also the first of the Latin apologists. His treatise *De cultu feminarum,* replete as it is with the influence of Juvenal, created a new genre of Christian hortatory literature in which cosmetic theology was addressed for the first time primarily to women. Tertullian ostensibly borrows the Stoic ethical criterion of virtue as life in accordance with nature only to alter it drastically in applying it to the female sex. At the outset the *De cultu feminarum* seems to proclaim Tertullian's allegiance to the Stoic norm of nature. Clothing dyed with precious colors is unnatural and hence immoral, he asserts; if God wanted wool to be blue or purple he would have created sheep with fleeces in those colors.[14] Similarly, warming to his subject, he charges that the use of cosmetics and hair dye by women is unnatural and impious as well as injurious to the health and an unsuccessful way of trying to mask one's age.[15] But Tertullian is not content to chastise women for the vanity or folly that inspires them to try to improve on nature. His main argument rests on the point that feminine beauty provokes masculine lust.[16] From a Stoic standpoint, if woman is beautiful by nature, her beauty is admissible and good. For Tertullian, on the other hand, women ought to be ashamed of their beauty. In trying to explain why, he refers to a Jewish apocryphal tradition according to which the angels, attracted by the charms of the daughters of men, copulated with them and taught them the arts of coquetry.[17] Women are morally at fault for having sinned with the fallen angels, and they ought to do penance for the attractions with which nature endows them. A modest appearance, without improvements superadded to nature, does not suffice for them. Rather, Tertullian says, women should take pains to conceal their natural attractions.[18] For women, it is not merely improving on nature that is immoral; in their case, nature as such is unacceptable as a moral criterion. More or less as an afterthought Tertullian also condemns men who enhance their natural appearance in order to appeal to women.[19] But he does not exhort men to a penitential cloaking of their masculine charms. For men, the norm of nature may be followed without hesitation, but for women this is not allowed.

For all its ostensible debts to Stoicism, Tertullian's argument in the *De cultu feminarum* ends by turning Stoic ethics inside out. He rejects a number of its central premises, such as the moral equality of men and women and the assessment of moral acts in terms of the agent's inner intentionality. Aiming his attack chiefly against women, he sees them as passive beings who can be defined in purely sexual terms. Their natural attributes are not important in their own right but only insofar as they cause men to act. Tertullian sees the natural condition of women as intrinsically flawed, not on account of any conscious choices they may have made but because of the inadvertent erotic effect that they have on the opposite sex. Men may sin when they improve on nature but women sin whether they improve on nature or adhere to it. Tertullian's cosmetic theology is a substantive departure from Stoic ethics. His *De cultu feminarum* reflects the influence of the antifeminist tradition in classical literature but its chief inspiration is an antifeminist attitude that goes back to a biblical, if apocryphal source, an attitude destined to have a long future ahead of it in Christian ascetic and hortatory literature.

The next Latin apologist to make an important contribution to the development of Christian cosmetic theology is St. Cyprian. Bishop of Carthage from 249 to 258, his high ecclesiastical office helps to account for the kind of interest in this theme that he reflects. Cyprian's *De habitu virginum* was addressed to a specific group of women in his diocese who had special pastoral requirements. In Cyprian's day the vocation of Christian monasticism had not yet developed in an institutionalized form. At the same time, the celibate calling was attracting to it a noticeable number of women. Consecrated virginity enabled them to respond to an ideal apostolic counsel and it also provided a dignified alternative to marriage. In writing a treatise advising consecrated virgins on how to comport themselves Cyprian was not speaking to a cloistered community of nuns who could rely on each other for group reinforcement under the rule of an abbess. Rather he wrote for individual celibate women who would remain at home, living with their families, but devoting themselves to prayer, devotional exercises, and ascetic practices. The stringency of his advice concerning hairstyles, makeup, and clothing takes account of the circumstances in which these women will be living as well as their virginal vocation. In its literary form Cyprian's *De habitu virginum* is modeled closely on Tertullian's *De cultu feminarum*. But Cyprian's scope and literary strategy are different. Where Tertullian wields the satirist's whip, heaping ridicule on the immodesty of female behavior in general through the device of invective. Cyprian concentrates on a positive portrayal of the method that he seeks to inculcate in a small but highly visible group of women, whose vocational commitment was a relatively unprecedented one in the history of Christianity up to that time. Despite the theological and pastoral dimensions of his approach, Cyprian expresses a much more genuinely Stoic respect than Tertullian does for the idea of nature as an ethical criterion. Most of his case is based on scriptural injunctions to womanly modesty, which he applied to the particular Christian calling of the women he addresses, personal adornment being especially unseemly for women vowed to celibacy. However, he does offer one argument based on the norm of nature. Cosmetics and hair dye, he notes, are immoral because they seek to improve on nature, which is an offense at once against the God who created nature and against the truth.[20]

If consecrated virgins were an important item on Cyprian's episcopal agenda, so was the schism mounted by his contemporary, Novatian (ca. 200-258). As the leader of a competing Christian community, Novatian confronted pastoral needs similar to those of Cyprian. He, too, produced a treatise on cosmetic theology aimed at women. It is, however, less narrow in its vocational focus than Cyprian's work and less preclusively dependent on Stoicism for the philosophy that informs it. Novatian's *De bono pudicitiae* is based on Tertullian's *De cultu feminarum*. Addressed to women, it argues that cosmetics, hair dye, and elaborate clothing sin against the modesty that guards chastity, adding that they are unnatural, an impious criticism of God's handiwork. However, Novatian departs both from Tertullian's penitential asceticism and from the Stoic norm of life in accordance with nature in adhering to the norm of moderation instead. Modesty, he states, can be defined as the avoidance of any form of extravagance, a decidedly Aristotelian criterion. Thus, he concludes, a moderate amount of self-enhancement is permissible.[21]

The first of the Latin church fathers, St. Ambrose (339-397), made a contribution of his own to the theme of cosmetic theology. To begin with, although he devoted considerable attention as a bishop and pastor to the vocations of marriage, virginity, and widowhood, these are not the contexts in which he discusses the topic. Nor does he devote a separate treatise to it. Cosmetic theology comes up only once in his oeuvre, and briefly, in his *Hexameron*. This is a theological treatise devoted to the nature of the universe, organized according to the Genesis account of the six days of creation. St. Basil had first developed this genre of Christian literature, and Ambrose's *Hexameron* is the first example of it in Latin. Another idea which he made accessible in Latin for the first time was the fourfold method of scriptural exegesis, pioneered by Philo Judaeus and Christianized by Origen. According to this technique, the biblical text yields a moral, a typological, and an anagogical meaning in addition to its literal sense. It is in connection with the moral exegesis of the creation story in Genesis that Ambrose develops the *topos* of cosmetic theology. Ambrose agrees that people should not try to alter or improve upon the image of God in themselves, a practice that would sin against truth while at the same time insulting the Creator and deceiving their fellow men. Like Tertullian and other previous Christian writers he addresses this exhortation primarily to women and their use of cosmetics, but not exclusively, although he does not specify what the analogous masculine failings might be. Ambrose's chief innovation in the handling of this topic lies in the fact that he does not approach it from the standpoint of either sexual ethics, the monastic vocation, or asceticism. Rather, he sees it as one among a larger group of moral problems which all involve deception, cruelty, or dishonesty in one way or another. A second new wrinkle in Ambrose's treatment of cosmetic theology is that he does not invoke the norm of nature in this connection, even though he raises the question in a treatise on the creation of the universe.[22]

Even more striking for its simultaneous dependence upon and independence from tradition is the approach to cosmetic theology taken by St. Jerome (ca. 347-420). Neither a pastor nor a systematic theologian, Jerome considered this subject out of his own personal interest. The way he handles it reveals the rhetorical style of argument he is wont to use in supporting ideas and persons of whom he approves and, even more, of attacking positions that he opposes. Jerome situates cosmetic theology in two contexts in which it had not been located before by Latin Christian writers, the vocation of widowhood and the attack on heretics. The first of these concerns was dear to Jerome's heart. It can be seen as an extension of Cyprian's application of cosmetic theology to the vocation of the consecrated virgin. In letters addressed to or about widows Jerome criticizes widows who wear elaborate clothing, cosmetics, and fashionable hairstyles. Apart from doing violence to nature, such practices, he says, are a sign of vanity and are even the mark of Antichrist. Since widows should not remarry, they should not seek to attract the admiration of men.[23] On another level Jerome's association of hair dye, cosmetics, and becoming clothes with Antichrist enables him to direct cosmetic theology against the Montanist heresy. Since Montanus' female associates accoutered themselves á la mode, he charges, they cannot have been true prophets.[24] While Jerome resorts here to an *ad feminam* argument whereby he challenges the truth claims of Montanism by casting aspersions on the modesty and chastity of Montanist women, his position also effects a reconstitution of the original rationale for cosmetic theology that the Stoics had developed and that Jerome's Christian predecessors had ignored as a function of their feminizing of this tradition. The Stoics judged the sage's presentation of self, whether conventional or unconventional, not only in terms of its consonance with nature but also in light of its effect on his credibility as a proponent of wisdom to the society around him. Although Jerome adheres to the feminization of cosmetic theology that had characterized the *topos* in Christian hands since Tertullian, his consideration of the Montanist women is noteworthy in that he treats them not only as sexual beings but as public persons equal to men in their social role as preachers and missionaries.

Jerome's perception of women as embodying the temptations of the flesh thus coincides with his ability to accept them as intellectual and spiritual beings on the same plane as men. In this latter sense he may even be regarded as the father of Christian feminism. In the pedagogical letters that he wrote to parents like Laeta and Gaudentius advising them on how to rear their daughters[25] and in his many letters to and about exemplary women Jerome makes his respect for women as the moral equals of men unequivocally clear. He sums up this position most forcefully in a letter to Principia where he warmly praises another woman, and by extension the addressee. For, as he says, "qui virtutes non sexu sed animo iudicamus."[26] Jerome's egalitarianism in this connection no doubt reflects his blending of the biblical principle that in Christ there is no male or female with the Stoic position on the equality of the sexes. He certainly shows the flexibility with which the Christian thinkers of the apologetic and patristic age could manipulate both the scriptural and classical sources that bore on the theme of cosmetic theology.

Even the few theologians subjected to study in this paper suggest the variety of approaches that were possible within the same basic Christian orientation. Pastoral need, personal inclination, and the stylistic or topical strategies dictated by the demands of hortatory or polemical rhetoric all help to explain the diverse viewpoints visible in the Christian transformations of Stoic cosmetic theology up through the time of St. Jerome. Subsequent research may reveal still other modifications of the theme by later patristic and medieval thinkers. Yet, by Jerome's day the fundamental Christianization and feminization—or antifeminization—of the theme had occurred. The materials had been prepared for the host of treatments of this *topos,* some serious and some not, from Tertullian's *De cultu feminarum* to Max Beerbohm's *The Pervasion of Rouge,* that were to follow in the sequel.

Oberlin College

NOTES

1. On the Cynics, see Donald R. Dudley, *A History of Cynicism from Diogenes to the 6th Century A.D.* (London: Methuen & Co. Ltd., 1937), esp. pp. 97-99, 100-03, 118-19, 199 for the Stoic borrowings.

2. *Stoicorum veterum fragmenta,* ed. H. F. A. von Arnim (Leipzig: B. G. Teubner, 1903-24), vol. I, p. 257 and vol. III, p. 253; Clement of Alexandria, *Stromateis* 4.8, ed. D. Nicolae le Nourry, *Patrologia graeca,* ed. J. P. Migne (Paris: 1857). Two good general treatments are Hans Reiner, "Die ethische Weisheit der Stoicker heute," *Gymnasium* 70 (1969), 330-51, and Geneviève Rodis-Lewis, *La morale stoïcienne* (Paris: Presses Universitaires de France, 1970). Other important studies of Stoic ethics exploring its connection with Stoic physics include Ernst Grumach, *Physis und Agathon in der alten Stoa* (Berlin: Weidmannsche Buchhandlung, 1932), pp. 1-43; G. B. Kerferd, "The Search for Personal Identity in Stoic Thought," *Bulletin of the John Rylands Library* 55 (1972), 177-96; A. A. Long, "The Stoic Concept of Evil," *Philosophical Quarterly* 18 (1968), 329-43; Otto Rieth, *Grundbegriffe der stoischen Ethik: Eine traditionsgeschichtliche Untersuchung* (Berlin: Weidmannsche Buchhandlung, 1933); Bohdan Wisniewski, "Sur les origines du *homologoumenos tê phusei zên des stoïciens,"* *Classica et Mediaevalia* 22 (1961), 106-16.

3. *SVF,* III, 215, 314, 317, 319, 333, 339; Seneca, *Ad Lucilium epistulae morales* 94.26, trans. Richard M. Gummere, Loeb Classical Library (London: William Heinemann Ltd., 1925-34); *Ad Marciam* 16.1-2, in *Moral Essays,* trans. John W. Basore, Loeb Classical

Library (London: William Heinemann Ltd., 1928–35); Cora E. Lutz, "Musonius Rufus, 'The Roman Socrates'," *Yale Classical Studies* 10 (1947), nos. 3–4, 12, pp. 38–48, 84–88. Good discussions of this topic are provided by Ludwig Edelstein, *The Meaning of Stoicism,* Martin Classical Lectures 21 (Cambridge, Mass.: Harvard University Press, 1966), pp. 73–75; Charles Favez, "Un féministe romain: Musonius Rufus," *Bulletin de la société des Etudes de Lettres de Lausanne* 8 (1933), 1–8; A. L. Motto, "Seneca on Women's Liberation," *Classical World* 66 (January 1962), 155–57. C. E. Manning, "Seneca and the Stoics on the Equality of the Sexes," *Mnemosyne,* ser. 4, 26 (1973), 170–77, argues unconvincingly that Seneca held women to be morally inferior to men.

4. Lutz, "Musonius Rufus," no. 21, p. 128; Epictetus, *The Discourses* 1.16, 3.1, trans. W. A. Oldfather, Loeb Classical Library (London: William Heinemann Ltd., 1926).

5. Seneca, *Ep.* 5.1–3.

6. Persius, *Saturae* 3.54, ed. W. V. Clausen (Oxford: Clarendon Press, 1966).

7. Ibid., 4.36–37.

8. Juvenal, *Saturae* 6.161–69, ed. W. V. Clausen (Oxford: Clarendon Press, 1966). The only woman he credits at all is the virgin Cloelia, who saved Rome from attack by swimming across the Tiber to alert the defenders, referred to in *Sat.* 3.60–61.

9. *Sat.* 2.47–48.

10. Ibid., 2.4–7.

11. Ibid., 2.11–13. This point has also been noted by Ludwig Friedlaender in the commentary in his edition of Juvenal (Amsterdam: Adolf M. Hakkert, 1962), p. 165.

12. *Sat.* 2.65.

13. Ibid., 2.16–17.

14. Tertullian, *De cultu feminarum* 1.8.2, ed. A. Kroymann, *Corpus christianorum, series latina* (Turnhout: Brepols, 1954). *Corpus christianorum* will be cited hereafter as *CC.*

15. *De cultu fem.* 2.5.2–4, 2.6.1–4.

16. Ibid., 2.21. One might contrast Tertullian here with the "beauty unadorned" theme found in classical love poems, in which the lady is enjoined by the speaker not to improve on nature because her natural attractions are sufficient or because she is more attractive au naturel, advice that is designed to emphasize her erotic appeal, not to minimize it. On this tradition see Archibald A. Day, *The Origins of Latin Love-Elegy* (Oxford: Basil Blackwell, 1938), pp. 39–47.

17. *De cultu fem.* 1.1.1–2. On this apocryphal tradition see Jean Danielou, *A History of Early Christian Doctrine before the Council of Nicaea,* trans. David Smith and John Austin Baker (London: Darton, Longman & Todd, 1977), III, pp. 164, 167.

18. *De cultu fem.* 2.2.5, 2.4.1.

19. Ibid., 2.8.1–3.

20. St. Cyprian, *De habitu virginum* 15.16, ed. G. Hartel, *Corpus scriptorum ecclesiasticorum latinorum* (Vienna: C. Geroldi, 1868). *Corpus scriptorum ecclesiasticorum latinorum* will be cited hereafter as *CSEL.*

21. Novatian, *De bono pudicitiae* 12.2–4, ed. G. F. Diercks, *CC* (Turnhout: Brepols, 1972).

22. St. Ambrose, *Exameron* 6.8.47, ed. Carolus Schenkl, in *Opera, CSEL* (Vienna: Holder-Pichler-Tempsky, 1897–1968).

23. St. Jerome, *Epistulae* 38.3.2, to Marcella; *Ep.* 54.7.1–3, to Furia, ed. Isidorus Hilberg, *CSEL* (Vienna: F. Tempsky, 1910–18).

24. St. Jerome, *De viris inlustribus* 40, ed. Carl Albrecht Bernoulli (Frankfurt: Minerva G. M. B. H., 1968).

25. *Ep.* 107.4–13, to Laeta; *Ep.* 128.1–3, to Gaudentius. On this topic see Johannes N. Brunner, *Der hl. Hieronymus und die Mädchenerziehung auf Grund seiner Briefe an Laeta*

und Gaudentius: Eine patristisch-pädagogische Studie (München: J. J. Lentnerschen Buchhandlung, 1910); Charles Favez, "Saint Jérôme pédagogue," *Mélanges de philologie, de littérature et d'histoire anciennes offerts à J. Marozeau* (Paris: Les Belles Lettres, 1948), pp. 173–81.

26. *Ep.* 127.5.3, to Principia. This point has been developed well by M. Turcan, "Saint Jérôme et les femmes," *Bulletin de l'Association Guillaume Budé* (1968), pp. 259–72. Turcan corrects the position of David Wiesen, *St. Jerome as a Satirist: A Study in Christian Latin Thought and Letters* (Ithaca: Cornell University Press, 1964), ch. 4 and p. 114, who notes only the antifeminist aspect of Jerome's treatment of women.

Masters of Suspense:
Argumentation and Imagination in
Anselm, Bernard, and Calvin

M. B. Pranger

*I*t is well known that the historiography of medieval philosophy was for a long time dominated by the view that the relationship between faith and reason was the major problem that beset medieval scholastics. There was a vague *communis opinio* among the commentators about the development of this problem in the Middle Ages which went something like this: Reason, which had been originally enclosed within the narrow confines of faith *(credo ut intelligam)* developed itself into a more or less independent entity through the impulse of Aristotelian philosophy; this tendency, so scholars argued, reached its zenith in the philosophy of Thomas Aquinas and subsequently went into an inevitable decline which was concluded in the *via moderna* and the inexorability of Ockham's "razor." This interpretation of the main significance of high medieval philosophy has now been replaced by a different perspective. A more accurate appreciation of the technicalities of the scholastic method has helped to uncover new problem areas. Scholarly interest has shifted to other topics especially in medieval logic and semantics. This intense preoccupation on the part of recent scholars with technical problems has by no means had adverse effects on the issue of the relation between faith and reason. More precisely, this dichotomy has been unmasked as an historiographically inexact category. Besides, and in addition, contemporary insights into the technical structure of language and logic have been of great benefit to the study of medieval theology and metaphysics proper.

Up to this point there seems to be no great problem. But difficulties do arise in consideration of the fact that the old interpretative model of "faith and reason" has been discarded in the effort to typify the technical methods as such in terms which encompass them. In this context it

15

would seem that in philosophy and theology the high Middle Ages has an advantage over the other medieval periods. The rather strict form of the educational process and its written reports *(Sententiae, quaestiones disputatae, summae)* guarantees a certain formal continuity to the philosophical and theological literature. But continuities are not as clear in the solution of the problems which were posited as they are in the manner in which these problems were posed. To give an example: although both Thomas Aquinas and William of Ockham speak of a causal chain, a causal chain for Thomas Aquinas is not the same as one for Ockham. But even though their substantive views are diametricallyrically opposed, the two thinkers use the same vocabulary and they can be compared to one another. This artificially intramural character of the scholastic method also limits the variety—however great it may in itself be—of solutions to theological problems discussed within that context. Even if an approach different from the discursive is taken, it is usually a mystical one in which the validity of the laws of discursive thought is not essentially challenged but rather transcended.

In noting this more or less formal continuity in high scholastic philosophy and theology, something negative has also been said. The problem here is not so much a difference between form and content as one which derives from the nature of the form itself. The relatively univocal character of the scholastic vocabulary ensures that the form into which a product of thought is molded does not have to be uniquely constructed, carved out ad hoc, or justified for that idea alone. The only *cloture* which plays a part here would be a postulate concerning the scope within which an argument has an unequivocal validity independent of what it encloses or excludes. Here the technique of thought, so to speak, creates its own bounds and framework.

It is exactly this one–dimensionality, this coincidence of framework and form, which makes the pressure of the scholastic method on earlier and later history and its theological and philosophical products so great and which *appears* to uncover the structure of these products. However, it would be shortsighted to give in to this pressure and to assume that one–dimensional, scholastic frameworks can make sense of earlier, later, or different contemporary currents of philosophy or religion. Of course, I do not mean to say that nonscholastic products of thought have no continuity. It is probably quite possible to sketch an outline of the *outillage mental* of eleventh and twelfth century theology and philosophy and of nonuniversity currents in the thirteenth and fourteenth century which reflects a nonscholastic but yet identifiable kind of continuity: didactic method, scriptural exegesis, philosophical tradition, literary and rhetorical forms and topoi afford one enough material.

Without doubt many thinkers can be found who can be placed and explained with reference to such an *outillage mental*. Yet, in periods of this kind the diffuseness and diversity are greater, and the way in which theological and philosophical texts are accommodated is more varied than what we might find within high scholasticism. As a result it is more difficult in these periods to construct diagonals unless one is content to connect texts from different levels with each other in a kind of jour-nalistic continuity.

The study that follows is designed to illustrate the fact that, from the eleventh to the sixteenth centuries, thinkers who addressed very simi-lar problems used widely divergent linguistic strategies and argument flowing from them. If, for instance, we are concerned with a text o Anselm in which (either according to the author or, as far as that goes according to his exegete or editor) the *ars dialectica* is applied to matter of faith, or if we are concerned with a text of Bernard in which such method is dismissed rigorously and antidialectically, this does not ne cessarily mean that the framework within which the text was produced and within which it can be understood coincides with the problem of the application or nonapplication of *dialectica*. First there is a much more fundamental problem: in the estimation of the author of the text, what kind of reality is the object to which *dialectica/logica* is to be applied? In other words, the question is that of the identity of things, as the author understands it and the method that he thinks is applicable to that reality. But this is exactly the point where the ways part. The scholastic method (or, for that matter, any philosophical approach claiming uni-versal validity) presupposes a broad view of reality; its model of explanation, for example, sets out chains of causality which help it to expand so that more and more of reality can be caught up in an ever more complicated web. However, a wide number of other possible definitions of these terms also exist. Many thinkers have a view of being and reality such that their thought would not be faithfully represented by explanatory models that tend to generalization of a scholastic type or, indeed, generalization as such.

In this paper the central problem is the concept of identit in Anselm of Canterbury, Bernard of Clairvaux, and John Calvir My approach will not be to try to demonstrate horizontal connections c genetic relations among these men. Rather, the texts analyzed will t treated as chains of argument, as clusters of ideas which are not nece sarily related directly to each other but which are alternative approache to the same basic issue. In this way I want to illustrate how each of thes thinkers thought on the basis of his own particular—and sometime self-created—idea of reality. If there is common ground for all three, is the strong belief in the identity of a reality which tends to regulate and reduce instead of expanding the chains of causality which it or its interpreters use.

This process of reduction or narrowing down tends to change the structure of argument and discussion for Anselm, Bernard, and Calvin. In each case stratification enters the picture and the *demonstrandum,* which in one-dimensional thought models is proved by the unambiguous rules of the game, here becomes suspense, a strategy involving the postponement of an identity whose status, and not only in the final analysis, depends on the power of its creator's imagination.

In a sense the present paper is meant to be an exercise in historiographical asceticism. Of course, it is possible to look for a theory of knowledge in Bernard, as Gilson does at the end of his *Theologie mystique de St. Bernard,*[1] but such a technique introduces a hidden point of comparison, that is, the very possibility, or rather the general existence, of a theory of knowledge. It is my intention to begin right at the other end. Since historical continuities or influences are not the point of this inquiry, the three figures treated will be presented in a thematic, not chronological order. My starting point is a small cluster of ideas in the thought of a single thinker, Calvin, whose concept of identity is dense to the extent of seeming unassailable from outside. The next section will treat Anselm, who allows for more room in playing his dialectical games—with the intention, however, of reducing them all to the beauty and joy of strict identity. The last section, on Bernard, will deal with a figure who seems to feel himself entitled to complete rhetorical liberty in order to impose his most personal idea of identity, and who is, as a consequence, beyond the reach of any one-dimensional interpretation whatsoever.

Our "ascetic" method naturally implies the absence of connecting texts between the three sections. There is simply nothing to be connected, at least not as long as we are faithful to the technique we have designed: imitating the texts we have selected, so to speak, we concentrate on condensation, on creating clusters of analysis as closely reasoned and self-consistent in their own terms as possible. If the void thus created from one cluster to the next still presupposes an element of comparison, then it rather should be called a vanishing point, or, to continue the ascetic terminology: a desert in which one hopes some roses will flourish.

II. The Extra-Calvinisticum

In order to put these matters into bold relief, I will, as announced, first discuss a text—an argument—by someone who is not medieval and whose philosophical affinities to and confidence in natural reason cannot be called great: John Calvin. In his *Institutio* he treats the theologico–philosophical problems which arise from the Calvinist doctrine of Christ's presence in the Eucharist. In opposition to the Lutheran doctrine of the ubiquity of Christ's resurrected body as the basis for rejecting transubstantiation, he posits the literal dimension of human nature as it is subject to the temporal created order and thus to the laws of thought: the so–called *extra-Calvinisticum*.[2] According to this view, Christ, who has been absent in the flesh since his Ascension, is present in the Eucharist not in the flesh but only in a spiritual manner. As Calvin puts it:

> For here it is not a question of what God could do, but what he willed to do. Now, we affirm that what was pleasing to him was done. But it pleased him that Christ be made like his brethren in all things except sin (Heb.4.15; cf. ch. 2.17). What is the nature of our flesh? Is it not something that has its own fixed dimension, is contained in a place, is touched, is seen? And why (they say) cannot God make the same flesh occupy many and diverse places, be contained in no place, so as to lack measure and form? Madman, why do you demand that God's power make flesh to be and not to be flesh at the same time! It is as if you insisted that he make light to be both light and darkness at the same time! But he makes light to be light; darkness to be darkness; and flesh, flesh. Indeed, when he pleases he will turn darkness into light and light into darkness; but when you require that light and darkness not differ, what else are you doing than perverting the order of God's wisdom? Flesh must therefore be flesh; spirit, spirit—each thing in the state and condition wherein God created it.[3]

Lux, lux, tenebrae, tenebrae, Light, light, darkness, darkness. This seems a rather uncomplicated philosophy—to quote Erasmus—a "simple and rustic way of saying things" ("simplex et rusticana veritas").[4] Rabelais is still using the semantics of this expression in an agrarian context when he allows the bishop of the Island of the Papimans to contextualize the deliciously juicy pears which he offers Pantagruel and his company in these words: "We are simple folk, as it pleased God to make us. We call figs figs, plums plums, and pears pears."[5] This Rabelais quotation is in fact a parody on a rather rattling and imaginative larger coherence *in casu catholico*. When he had been asked about the meaning of the poorly painted portrait which these Papimans idolized, the same bishop had replied: "It is the archetype of that good God upon earth whose coming we devotedly await, and whom we hope to see one day in our land."[6] The meaning of "celluy Dieu," whose arrival is being anticipated with such fervor, is not, as the formula suggests, Christ, but rather the pope, who by his image is present but actually remains corporally absent.

Now Calvin. *Caro* as *caro, lux* as *lux, tenebrae* as *tenebrae:* none of this is meant as a parody, that much is certain. God desires the light to be light; that is to say, without counterinformation—as in the form of miracles—the logical laws of thought (identity and contradiction) are valid according to diving decree. This would seem to be a very literal understanding of the reality in question. The identity of things stands fast. In the present context this means that if Christ has taken on human flesh and is no longer present on earth, then with regard to that flesh he must be somewhere else and his return must be awaited as the arrival of a "Dieu de bien en terre" who resides in a place far away. In more Calvinistic terms: Christ is present in the spirit (symbolically in bread and wine) but according to the flesh he is in heaven as the pledge of what is to come.

What then is so extraordinary about this train of thought? Its great simplicity and its literal nature? Surely not in themselves. Many "rustic" arguments can be put forth, which for the rest have no very far-reaching consequences. In this case, however, the epistemological and semantic significance of *caro caro, lux lux* is great, even so great that whatever is offered as a framework or a limitation stands in danger of being destroyed or cut off by it. More concretely: although Calvin's theology is not antiphilosophical in the sense that he rejects general principles of thought, still his method of using these principles *(non simul esse et non esse)* not only makes logic as a pure *ars* impossible but also stands in the way of a reasoned analysis of what has been determined by divine decree. Calvin does not use a separate auxiliary language—like the scholastics—to support the structure of his theological system or, at least, to illuminate it. He attacks the position he rejects precisely by reducing it to the ordinary literal *usus loquendi*. The identity of things stands fast. Wherever that is the case—in other words, when there is reasoning at all—the terms of the argument must be univocal to the point of being identical with the contents of that reasoning; consequently the suspense of the argument is defined out of existence.

It is obvious that Calvin's reasoning in our fragment is not without consequence for the status of religious language. The medieval multi-layered exegetical system has been radically "pruned" by Calvin's "literalism." As a result there is no means by which the language of Scripture, or religious language in general, can be distinguished from other uses of language. For Calvin the *sola scriptura* principle takes itself literally in a very strict sense and as a consequence does not even permit itself to function as a logical-dialectical tool or as a framework.

The chain of argument of the *extra-Calvinisticum* is thus not as artless or without methodological implications as it may appear on first sight. Of course there is a continuum, a context within which matters can be discussed on their own level and compared, but the question arises as to whether this continuum is really impermeable and completely self-contained or whether it can be broken through somewhere. Are those things which do not clearly belong to this context excluded beforehand by Calvin so that his theology is made to appear more coherent than it factually is? Well, first there is the spiritual (omni-) presence of Christ which is symbolically expressed in the Sacrament. But it is exactly the postulate of the spiritual character of Christ's presence which absolves theologians (Calvin) from the problem of having to account for it within the chain of argument of the *extra-Calvinisticum,* because it is not an intrinsic part of that chain of argument thanks to Calvin's definition of his terms. The only suspense which Calvin has constructed is that of the absence of Christ in the flesh. To phrase it in the terms of the argument itself: Christ, whose advent is expected in the flesh, is excluded on the grounds of the employed principle of identity (continuum): it is impossible to expect of God *ut carnem faciat simul esse et non esse carnem.*

This is not the place to expound on how this suspense (theologically speaking: the elusive, the *promissio*-character of this Christology) carries the inherent danger of splitting the idea of identity (and its subject, too) *ad infinitum.* This again would create a no-man's-land, a living and thinking "space" in which the subject of reality and imagination can function in no other than a broken and truncated way. Here it is enough to say that the chain of argument which has been analyzed can in no other way be constructed or "framed" except by a dubious and ambiguous use of what has been excluded in the first instance. Reference may be made by comparison to the *Heidelberg Cathechism,* which distinguishes the two natures of Christ and at the same time unites them.[7] The argument is that, because the Godhead can be enclosed by nothing and is omnipresent, it follows that this same Godhead is outside the humanity it has accepted and yet is in it and remains personally united to it. *Simul esse et non esse:* this would seem to be the price which has to be paid for the identity of Christ.

III. The Extra-Diabolicum

The next cluster that I want to examine is Anselm's argument on the fall of the Devil, which could be called the *extra-Anselmianum* or better still the *extra-diabolicum.*[8] Be it less agrarian and physical in nature, the core of this argument is as simple, condensed, and obvious as Rabelais's pears and Calvin's *caro*. As Anselm puts it in his dialogue *De casu diaboli:* "In like manner, just as nothing but good comes from the highest good, so nothing but being comes from the highest being and just as every good comes only from the highest good, so every being comes only from the highest being. Moreover, since the highest good is the highest being, it follows that every good is a being, and every being is a good. Therefore, just as nothing and not-being are not beings, so they are also not good. And thus, nothing and not-being are not from God, because from God come only being and good" (ch. 1). The disciple of the dialogue understands the argument well and "closes" the almost tautological discussion thus: "I now see clearly that being and good come only from God, and that only being and good come from God."

This mini-cluster of ideas çould well be left aside if it were not that it functions as a kind of continuum and one that Anselm situates within language itself. Language, of course, what Anselm calls *usus loquendi* (language in general: either that of faith or that of everyday speech) can be used for all purposes of expression. What holds this diffuse totality together and transposes it into an actual form is truth in the sense in which it has been "syllogistically closed" in our cluster. "Watch out lest you should think that I am denying the thing on account of which Scripture says that God does cause evil or not-being; or that I would find fault with someone if he, following the use of Scripture, were to say this. But we shouldn't so much cling to inappropriate words which conceal the truth, as we should seek to discover the genuine truth which is hidden under the many types of expression" (ch. 1).

Anselm's remark allows at least two conclusions. First, there is no special language structure (e.g., an *ars dialectica*) which can be applied to the *usus loquendi*. A corrective continuum, so to say, has been built into language itself and thus allows for no getaways. Anselm's language here has as little use for a technical framework as Calvin's. Second, this cluster is almost exclusively composed of "elastic" propositions: being is being, nothing is nothing, being is not nothing. If Anselm's language actually functions as a continuum then one of two things may be true: in seeking to define more exactly the underlying and hidden truth, possibilities are soon eliminated *or* a closed, almost tautological, situation is applied to the undetermined and uncorrected *usus loquendi* in order to give it a more sophisticated dimension and stratification.

On the basis of this point of view I wish to examine Anselm's argumentation in *De casu diaboli.* In this dialogue Anselm attempts to explain the fall of the Devil by using the pair of terms "to give" and "to receive." The scriptural phrase "quid habes quod non accepisti" is the foundation of Anselm's discussion. From this he derives a technical formula: *dare semper causa accipiendi* ("to give is always the cause of to receive"). This in itself presents no problem. However, the negation of this proposition gives more food for thought: *non dare cause non accipiendi* ("not giving is the cause of not receiving") would acquit the Devil, who has not received the grace of perseverance, of the guilt of his fall. For this reason Anselm seeks a solution, a new possibility: *Potest enim non dare non esse causa non accippiendi* ("It is possible that not giving is not the cause of not receiving"). In this case the blame for not receiving is not necessarily on the Giver even if it were true that giving is always the cause of receiving. The solution lies in an examination of the one who has not received (the Devil). What is it that gives him the capacity of not receiving? What is the *potestas non accipientis?*

The not-receiving of the Devil, according to the student in the dialogue, is preceded by an absence of will or ability which on their part presupposes a capacity of perseverance; otherwise there would be no possibility of sin (ch. 3). Nothing extraordinary so far. A complication however does appear when Anselm refuses to accept the conclusion that the Devil, disposing of the will and ability to receive perseverance, factually has received and has persevered. Neither will nor ability function a priori in that sense. In order to understand the true meaning of will and ability, Anselm postulates a provisional goal which makes it possible to view the process of will and ability, including their possible interruption, as a whole. The result is a remarkably empirical description of will and ability which in principle does not leave room for unwillingness and inability. "Have you ever begun anything with the will and ability to complete it, but did not complete it because your will was changed before you finished?" Anselm asks the student. "S: Frequently. A: So you willed and were able to persevere in what you did not persevere. S: I certainly willed to do so, but I did not perservere in the willing, and therefore I did not persevere in the action" (ch. 3). As far as the will is concerned one might regress *ad infinitum*. During this digression the will and the object of will diverge more and more. A cause for this deficiency (i.e., not-willing) must be found which breaks through the regression. Anselm realizes this demand by expressing the problem in final terms: one failure is not willing (something) to the end *(non pervoluit)*. As applied to the Devil the conclusion runs as follows: "the Devil, who received the will and ability to receive perseverance and the will and ability to persevere, did not receive perseverance and did not persevere because he did not will it to the end."

Of course this explanation is far from complete, or perhaps rather more than complete. For the *per* ("to the end") has to save both the proposition from an insoluble contradiction *(velle = non-velle)* and the argument from a *regressus ad infinitum.* Now, one of two things must obtain: either the will or ability to receive or the not-willing to the end *(non-pervelle)* has to be eliminated since it is difficult to see how will and ability make sense where completion has already been achieved. In other words: *pervelle* does not mean much more or less than the actual confirmation of the fact: he has persevered *(pervoluit).* What then is the meaning of its negation: *non pervelle?* Does it still contain elements of will and ability? It is obvious that the *per* must be differentiated; in terms of *posse/velle:* at stake it is not the will which the Devil had when he really willed, but the will which he did not have when he did not will. Is there a possibility of "breaking" this merely negative state of affairs other than reducing the whole chain of argument (i.e., the ultimate not-receiving of the Devil) to the author of all completion *(per),* who is the Eternal Giver?

It is through a metaphor that Anselm creates "space" between the *velle* and the *pervelle:* "For example, suppose there is a miser who wants to keep his money, yet prefers to have bread, which he is not able to have unless he gives up some of his money. He wills to give up (or desert) some of his money before he is unwilling to keep it, but he is unwilling to keep it (only) because he must give it up to get bread" (ch. 3). In chapter 4 this metaphor is interpreted as well as unmasked in terms of the actual subject of the dialogue. The bread which is preferred by the miser is replaced by either *iustitia* or a *commodum.* The latter is circumscribed as: *ex commodis enim constat beatitudo, quam vult omnis rationalis natura.* Now the Devil has preferred a *commodum* to *iustitia;* "he extended his will beyond justice by a disordered *(inordinate)* willing of something that was more than he has received." What else can be found beyond *ordo* and *iustitia?* Willing something different, the Devil has willed the impossible. Since *ordo* is related to God, the only one whose nature is such that nothing else can be conceived to be like him, the Devil, by willing *inordinate* has in fact willed nothing at all. As a result the scheme of *commodum* as happiness which is desired by every rational nature breaks down and so does the metaphor of the miser. As a matter of fact the *non-accipiens* has willed nothing, has received nothing and nothing has been given to him. In the course of the dialogue Anselm will use the same unstable happiness again in order to elucidate the ultimate happiness (as *iustitia);* an *iustitia* which, on account of its absolute nature, is the cause of the empty, relative, and arbitrary character of the common concept of *beatitudo.*

In spite of this provisional differentiation of *pervelle,* we still face the question of the *potestas non-accipientis.* After all, what we are looking for is not a weak and relative *potestas* which is enclosed within the ultimate completion of empirical facts but the *propria potestas* of the Devil, in other words, his disposition to will or not to will, which, in case of not-willing, is not immediately reduced to nothing.

As one might expect, the argument is developed in an initially misleading direction. Anselm seems to admit that preceding the existence or nonexistence of facts there is a natural *potestas* of will: "No one is compelled by fear or a sense of any disadvantage, nor attracted by love or any benefit, to will any particular thing, unless he first has the natural will, or inclination, to avoid what is disadvantageous and to enjoy what is beneficial. By this natural will he moves himself to other willings" (ch. 12). Indeed, this is a natural ability of the will, but how does it work? In order to "move" *("movere")* this ability, one is supposed to will first; however, "he [i.e., the Devil] who has never yet willed anything is able to will nothing through himself." Consequently, the Devil who was predisposed to have a will, but actually wills nothing, does not have a *prima voluntas a se,* that is, does not have *potestas.* So to be able to will is to will something. Here Anselm reintroduces the example of *beatitudo,* happiness without *iustitia* which is desired by every rational creature, including the unjust. Provisionally the universality of this happiness guarantees the position of *potestas.* Subsequently this general human desire is connected with the nature of the human subject: "For no one wants any particular thing unless he thinks *(sibi putat)* it will be beneficial *(commodum)* to him in one way or another *(aliquo modo)*." This happiness can be more distinctly specified: "I am talking about this happiness because nobody can be happy who does not want happiness (in general); and no one can be happy by having what he does not want or by not having what he does not want" (ch. 12). Thanks to the universality of the *beatitudo* there seems to be plenty of room for *posse.* This happy state of affairs does not last long, however. Another démasqué reveals the unique and exclusive meaning of *beatitudo* which, interpreted in a strict sense, turns the *sibi putat* into an empty, merely subjective way of thinking. Application of comparative notions such as *maior, verius,* and *altius* leads to the real, objective *beatitudo* which is willed by a just will. *Iustitia* appears to be true reality, *aliquid* and the only possible object and *potestas* of will. The final decision concerning the status of this *potestas* can be taken only on the basis of final reality, completion, facts. Consequently, notwithstanding its universality, the *beatitudo* of the *commodum* (a *quasi-aliquid)* cannot offer a ground for *potestas.*

Why then did the Devil fall? "S: But why did he will what he was supposed not to will? A: No cause preceded this willing except his mere ability to will. S: Then he willed to desert justice because he was able to will? A: No, because the good angel was also able to will, but he did not will to desert justice. For no one wills what he is able to will simply because he is able to will; there must be still another cause—although, of course, he would never will anything at all if he were not able to will. S: Why, then, did he will? A: Only because he willed. For there was no other cause by which his will was in any way driven or drawn; but his will was both its own efficient cause and its own effect—if such a thing can be said!" (ch. 27).

Remarkable guile, yet again! *Potestas* no more than seems to be the only cause of the will. But this is not the case. For the good angel, although in the position to will like the Devil, did not behave that way. In this case it was his goodness which, as an *alia causa* ("still another cause"), preceded his good being and as such determined his *potestas*. Accordingly, the *potestas* of the Devil can never be sufficient ground for his not-willing. Why then did the Devil (not) will? Because he did (not) will. Cause and effect circle around actuality without being interrupted by any separate *potestas* whatsoever. But the démasqué is not yet complete. There still seems to be a *potestas* which precedes the will; for whatever is—and the will is supposed to be "something somehow"—is good, should be good and as such originates from God. In a very wide perspective Anselm gives a place to a *potestas* of the Devil. But, however indirectly, this *potestas,* in the final analysis, depends on God, of whom it can be said that he has given what he has permitted to be taken. Standing as the Eternal Giver at the beginning and the end, God alone is responsible, not for this theft as such, but for the distance, the room, and the perspective in which the theft is committed.

This is the note in which *De casu diaboli* ends. What have we achieved? All but a ground for the *potestas non-accipientis.* Yet this fascinating analysis of what was not possible and in fact did not exist, has evoked, straight through the common language, an image of what really is: *aliquid, iustitia, beatitudo, deus.* Without doubt, an *extra-diabolicum.* Anselm's application of his principle of identity *(iustitia = aliquid)* has condensed the so spaciously constructed chain of causality *(potest enim non dare non . . . .).* As such, he has succeeded in excluding the Devil through a finely attuned process of elimination. In the same process Anselm has succeeded in eliminating every suggestion of causal relationship and explanation in the area of non-willing and *non-ratio.* But what kind of wasteland remains on the other side of this tautological identity! The Devil: here is the territory of *malum, nihil, non.* But it is specifically the *non* that has no claim at all to its own existence because it has already been claimed in the terms of the tautology. As a result not–willing and inability are always confronted with and resolved in *aliquid* or *iustitia.* One could well ask whether the distinction between the nondiscursive, unstructured territory of the Devil and that of *tautological* identity *(aliquid)* is as great as it appears.

"Nous sommes gens simples et appellons . . ." Everything depends on the form given to this "tautology" and on what name is used to describe it. What the Anselmian *extra–diabolicum,* in any event, does not do is give an extra guarantee of how the form appears. There is no causal coherence which would support such an attempt. Causal coherence at the most is a continually changing perspective (what Anselm calls *diverso intuitu),* the fine distinction between thought and reality, the not so very massive monastery wall, the self–created cloture which does not achieve form but by artful excisions: the suspense of the inventive (imaginative) not willing and not receiving of the Devil.

IV. Bernard and His Ego

After the preceding analysis it should hardly be surprising that Anselm, on being confronted with the famous question of whether the Devil had become the rightful possessor of man after his Fall from Paradise—an indenture which only God's sovereign mercy could redeem—answers in the negative. As far as the language of the *usus loquendi* is concerned, the Devil to a certain extent can act as he pleases and torment man *iuste* with God's permission or at least tolerance. In the proper sense, *proprie,* however, Anselm would say that there is no case to be made for this *ius.* There would be no way to make such a case for someone with as shaky a ground for existence as the Devil. Conclusion: "For this reason we must believe that by this 'handwriting' no justice whatsoever of the devil can be found in the vexation of man. Therefore, in the same way as in the good angel, there is no injustice at all, so in the evil angel there is no justice whatsoever. Therefore there is no reason why God should not use his strength against the devil in order to liberate man" *(Cur deus homo* I.7).[9]

This very point was taken up from Anselm by Peter Abelard in his *Commentary* on the *Epistle to the Romans:* "Therefore it seems for this reason that the devil who has seduced man has acquired no right in seducing him, unless perhaps, so to say, in so far as the Lord's permission pertains; He who has delivered him over to punishment (by the Devil) as to a gaolor and torturer."[10] Among the many arguments and problems with which he was concerned, Bernard of Clairvaux, it is known, also discussed this point, emphasizing that he had been incited to do so by his friend, William of St. Thierry. A report of the great debate between the antagonists Bernard and Abelard at the Council of Sens in 1140 can be found in Bernard's *Letters* 189 and 190.[11] Although this report is primarily literary it affords enough material for a philosophical analysis.

It is my intention to consider a part of Bernard's argument—that of the rights of the Devil with regard to man—as a chain of argument and in this way to show its structure and framework. As such this framework is quite straightforward. In the same way that Anselm eliminates the will and the right of the Devil as a dialectical impossibility, Bernard introduces both as a rhetorical necessity. First, however, I want to discuss the framework within which Bernard expresses his very personal indignation.

The point of departure is the fragment which was quoted from Abelard's *Commentary*. In this fragment, Abelard turns himself *expressis verbis* against a *communis opinio* originating with the Church Fathers. First, Bernard is angry and indignant that Abelard is so impudent as to think that he knows better than tradition teaches:

> What shall I judge more intolerable in these words? Blasphemy or arrogance? What more damning, the temerity or the impiety? Or is it rather more just to punch in the mouth someone who speaks in this manner than to argue against him rationally? Doesn't he rightly provoke the hands of all against himself whose hands are against all? He says: the others yes, me no. And you then? Can you put something better forward? Can you find something more subtle? Is there something more secret which has been revealed to you alone you can boast of, which has passed by so many saints and fled wise men? (*Ep.* 190.V.11)

Then Bernard continues with the framework of Holy Scripture and the *doctores* which, he claims, Abelard alone pointedly ignores:

> Say then, tell us what this is, what you see and no other else. Or has the Son of God not become man in order to liberate him? You alone seem to think that, no one else. All right, you can view the matter as you like. You have not received this (however) from a wise man, not from a prophet, nor from the Apostle and certainly not from the Lord himself. The Master of the gentiles has received from God what he has delivered to us. The Master of all admits that his doctrine is not his. I do not speak, he says, through myself. You, however, give us something from your own, what

you have received from no one. Whosoever speaks falsely, speaks of himself. Keep your own things to yourself. I listen to the prophets and the apostles, I obey the Gospel, but not the Gospel according to Peter. Do you found a new Gospel? The Church has not received a fifth Gospel. What else evangelize the Law, the Prophets, the Apostles, the apostolical men to us, than what you alone deny, i.e., that God made man in order to liberate man? And if an Angel from heaven gives us a different Gospel, he be damned. (*Ep.* 190.V.12)

This is clear and understandable language! For Bernard the Scriptures and the Fathers form a continuum which guarantees Truth. They form a continual chain that can be disrupted only from the outside by someone who, like Anselm's Devil, has received something from no one and who—*de suo*—places himself outside this chain as an interfering element, who speaks falsely. The remainder of Bernard's argument is completed within this *sic*-chain.

Scriptural proof follows: in high gear Bernard quotes a number of passages which he assumes evidently concern the Devil and his power. In fact these passages name the Devil directly only in a few cases. Of course, Bernard's procedure is not uncommon, but he is a past master of making the most of it in order to expand his argument to its very rhetorical limits. "And that they may recover themselves out of the snare of the Devil, who are taken captive by him at his will" (II Tim.2.25) is the clearest and most direct text in favor of the Bernardian position. But the others? "Whom he hath redeemed from the hand of the enemy" (Ps. 106.2; Vg.); "Who hath delivered us from the power of darkness, and hath translated us into the kingdom of his dear Son" (Col.1.13); and the finest and most indirect one: "Thou couldest have no power at all against me, except it were given thee from above" (John 19.11)—Jesus speaking to Pilate, as to a "member of the Devil" *("qui membrum erat diaboli")* (*Ep.* 190.V.12).

The remainder of Bernard's argument is built on the principle of rhetorical symmetry and in a style of not naming things directly but of speaking allusively. Bernard suggestively conjures up a dark past in which things have gone wrong and which forms the necessary occasion for the luminous but ever mysterious appearance of Christ. "It is another who constitutes the sinner than he who justifies from sin: one by seed, one by blood. Or is sin to be found in the seed of the sinner, and not justice in the blood of Christ? But justice, so he would say, belongs to its owner, and what then to you *(quid ad te)*? It be so. But sin also belongs to its owner, what then to me *(quid ad me)*?" (*Ep.* 190,VI,16).

If we put the question to what extent Bernard is using rational argument
here, we could answer that one *causa* (sin, the Devil's *potestas)* is
confronted with the other *causa (iustitia Christi)*. But there is no inkling
of a discursive articulation of a chain of argumentation. As far as that
goes, it appears that we are here confronted with one great unarticulated
area of the Devil, an unlimited religious–scriptural continuity, which is
not interrupted by any kind of *aliquid*. Where then is the suspense,
if any?

Sed iustitia, inquiet . . . quid ad te? . . . quid ad me? These are the
final words of an intermezzo in which for a moment the rhetorical
symmetry of Bernard's expostulation is slightly deflected and suspended before it again is continued in full force. The situation appears
to be rather muddled and absurd: Bernard concludes this passage with
an imaginary objection by Abelard *(inquiet)* which is not only the exact
opposite of what he (and also Anselm) actually thought but which also
gives rise to the suspicion that Bernard has covertly bypassed Anselm as
well as Abelard in the problem at stake—the elimination of extra-
human and extra–divine human elements from the process of salvation.
What has happened? First there is the Colossian text which is already
found in Anselm's *Cur deus homo:* "Blotting out the handwriting of
ordinances that was against us, which was contrary to us, and took it out
of the way, nailing it to his cross; And having spoiled *[exspolians]*
principalities and powers, he made a shew of them openly, triumphing
over them in it" (Col.2.14, 15). Association with the *exspolians* now
brings Bernard to a number of "personal" considerations:

> Utinam ego inveniar in his spoliis, quibus spoliatae sunt con-
> trariae potestates, traductus et ipse in possessionem Domini. Si
> me insecutus Laban arguerit, quod recesserim clam ab eo, audiet
> clam me accessisse ad eum, et ob hoc clam recessisse. Subiecit me
> illi causa secretior peccati, subduxit me illi ratio occultioris iusti-
> tiae. (*Ep.* 190.VI.6)

> [I wish I could be found in these spoils of battle, spoils which have
> destroyed the mighty—and be translated and that in the posses-
> sion of the Lord! If Laban had argued on following me that I had
> left him secretly, let him hear from me that it was in secret that I
> came to him, and that for this reason I left him secretly. I was
> subjugated to him by a more secret reason of sin, and I was led
> away from him by reason of a more hidden justice.]

This passage deserves some further remarks. Important here is the *me*
of *si me insecutus,* a *me* fenced in by two *clams,* two hidden causes.

"Personal" considerations were just mentioned. From a stylistic point of view this can hardly be taken to mean that Bernard suddenly is making a subjective move and to that extent becomes "personal." We are not concerned with that kind of *me;* the argument and the place of *me* is much too carefully and meticulously structured for such superficiality.

In this passage, however, there is a noteworthy elimination which suddenly concentrates what in the first instance is such a loosely constructed chain of causality (or the rhetorical construction which is so much like it) into a miniscule totality. *Si me insecutus Laban:* Bernard regards Laban as an especially suitable candidate to figure as a *membrum diaboli.* The other party is not identified by name: Jacob has been directly replaced by *me* seemingly without any rhetorical or contextual justification. This same *me* is then surrounded by mystery *(clam, causa secretior).* Not only are questions about the past eliminated, they are not even permitted; to use the words of Thomas Mann's Felix Krull, whose famous dialogue with the military doctor in many ways affords a marvelous comparison with the Bernardian literary technique in the passage under consideration: "es war mir, es müsse ein Geheimnis bleiben" ("it seemed to me that it would have to remain a secret"). This mystery stands in flagrant opposition to the turbulent exuberance with which Bernard until here has discussed the *potestas* of the Devil and the *iustitia Christi* as if they presented no mystery to him at all. The effect of our passage on the preceding and the following text by Bernard is bound to be great. The suspense which Bernard has introduced in the form of *me* and the mystery of *clam* codifies, as it were, the language which surrounds this passage and its rhetorical constructions as an area which is purposely not articulated and thus retains its momentum: the whole text is held in the suspense of *me,* a *me* that can suddenly without announcement strike. It is this tension which creates an enormous distance from a one-dimensional dogmatic treatment of themes about the might and power of the Devil and the right and justice of Christ. Every discussion of these themes now stands in the sign of the *quid ad me* and the *quid ad te.* And Bernard does not mean appropriation; we may go so far as to say that even identification is too weak a description of what Bernard is saying.

Ego, here, without doubt, cannot but have a very strong form, not to say a strong realization of its identity if it is to succeed not only in keeping the territories of the Devil and of the *iustitia Christi* apart but also in distinguishing one *causa secretior* from the other. One is reminded of the enchanting trout streams and rivulets running near so many of Bernard's monasteries, which as two *causae occultiores* can be used to signify the waters of Urchaos as well as those of Paradise.

Lux, lux, tenebrae, tenebrae, caro, caro: Bernard's procedure is rather less simple and straightforward. There is no question here of a pre-given or pre-supposed or pre-ordained identity—certainly not in Bernard's idea of the meaning of *ego* in the text just examined. Consequently there is no system of logical or dogmatic principles which would make it possible to discuss its identity. Is the only conclusion we can reach that Bernard's reproach of Abelard in fact applies equally to himself? *Qui loquitur mendacium de suo loguitur.* However this may be, for using this code and keeping it internally coherent, for the application of *sic* and *non* in this apparently marshy land, one would seem to need some foothold, some *mendacium* certainly, some power of imagination at least.

University of Amsterdam

NOTES

*Translated from the Dutch by A. J. Vanderjagt. To him and to Professor Marcia Colish I am much indebted for support and criticism.

1. E. Gilson, *La theologie mystique de saint Bernard* (Paris: Vrin, 1947), p. 173.

2. For basic literature dealing with the *extra-Calvinisticum,* see: H. A. Oberman, "Die 'Extra'-Dimension in der Theologie Calvins," in *Geist und Geschichte der Reformation* (Berlin: Walter de Gruyter, 1966), and E. David Willis, *Calvin's Catholic Christology: The Function of the So-called Extra-Calvinisticum in Calvin's Theology* (Leiden: Brill, 1966).

3. John Calvin, *Institutes of the Christian Religion,* IV, 17, 24, ed. John T. McNeill, trans. Ford Lewis Battles, Library of Christian Classics, XXI (Philadelphia: Westminster Press, 1960), II, p. 1391.

4. Erasmus, *Adagia* 1205, in *Opera Omnia,* ed. J. Clericus, vol. II. (Leiden, 1703), col. 485-86.

5. Bk. 4, ch. 54. *Gargantua and Pantagruel,* trans. J. M. Cohen (New York: Penguin Books, 1955). French text: "Nous sommes simples gens, puysqu'il plaist à Dieu. Et appellons les figues figues, les prunes prunes, et les poires poires."

6. Ibid., ch. 50. French text: "C'est l'idée de celluy Dieu de bien en terre, la venue duquel nous attendons devotement et lequel esperons une foys veoir en ce pays."

7. *Heidelberg Catechism,* Sunday 17, question 48.

8. *De casu diaboli, S. Anselmi Cantuariensis Archiepiscopi Opera Omnia,* ed. F. S. Schmitt, vol. I, pp. 227-76. The English translations from *De casu diaboli* are taken from: Jasper Hopkins and Herbert Richardson, *Truth, Freedom and Evil: Three Philosophical Dialogues by Anselm of Canterbury* (New York: Harper and Row, 1967).

9. *Opera Omnia,* vol. II, p. 59.

10. *Petri Abaelardi Commentaria in Epistolam Pauli ad Romanos,* II (III, 26), *Corpus Christianorum, Continuatio Mediaevalis* XI (Turnhout, 1969), p. 115.

11. *S. Bernardi Opera,* vol. VIII, *Epistolae,* ed. J. Leclercq and H. Rochais, pp. 17–40. In these letters, written to Innocence II, Bernard urges the pope to condemn the "heresies" of Abelard.

Genre and Code in Abelard's
Historia Calamitatum

Mark Amsler

*T*he story of Abelard and Heloise has become one of the key romantic episodes in Western culture. It has helped produce our models of how men and women should act toward one another and the values to which they should subscribe. It has also been a focal point of the ongoing debate between life and art, between the representation of human relationships as they are and as we would like to think they are. The romantic legend, which probably dates from the early thirteenth century,[1] recapitulates in part the situation in Greek New Comedy, with the two young lovers separated by the girl's malevolent relative. In the romantic version, sincere, indestructible passion is the touchstone by which the quality of the love is measured. On the other side, however, are those who question the authenticity of the letters upon which the legend is based. For some, the letters are too sensual and sinful to be completely factual; for others, they are too exemplary to be true.[2]

But one important thing remains—the letters themselves. We still read the letters, especially the *Historia Calamitatum,* and for the time of the reading we do not question their authenticity. The debate about their truth or fiction is a red herring as far as our understanding of the *Historia*'s narrative transformations is concerned. No one doubts that the text is somehow based on specific historical events. But those events are given a certain shape in the *Historia* which depends less on their historicity than on the interrelations of the narrative elements. The *Historia* as a narrative experience is as true as Geoffrey of Monmouth's history, Boswell's biography, or *Jane Eyre.* Our analysis, therefore, will focus on the formal and generic features which direct our reading and shape us into the competent readers of his life which Abelard wants us to be. But interpretation always requires that the interpreter situate himself or herself with reference to the competencies the text presupposes.

A text, a verbal syntagm, is positioned atop a set of conventions and previously realized forms. Conventions are part of the writer's repertoire as well as devices which the reader uses to gain the experience of a text. Medieval texts rely on such verbal structures, or codes, because of the frequently anonymous and communal composition of texts during the period. In sociolinguistic terms, a code is a set of predictable or appropriate utterances. At the same time, a code is the pattern of transformations by which a discrete perception or experience can be articulated in a culturally or communally accepted language. We might cite Roland Barthes' metaphorical description here: "The code is a perspective of quotations, a mirage of structures . . . the units which have resulted from it (those we inventory) are themselves, always, ventures out of the text . . . they are so many fragments of something that has always been *already* read, seen, done, experienced; the code is the wake of that *already* . . . each code is one of the forces that can take over the text (of which the text is the network), one of the voices out of which the text is woven."[3]

But the codes which exist theoretically at the social level of language also make up the individual speaker's or writer's verbal materials. To varying degrees they constitute the givens, the "truths" of a particular speaker, and so mark out the degree of his or her participation in certain ideologies and accepted cultural values. These codes also enable a writer, consciously or unconsciously, to produce a text which is not so much a monistic, organic unity of form as a tissue of languages interwoven to generate a set of significances. In some texts these codes remain disjunct, thereby producing a discrepancy within the text which calls attention to unresolved tensions, ideological conflicts, generic inappropriateness, or misplaced emphasis. In other texts the tissue of codes generates significant relationships between parts of the text. These relations define the center of the text's essential concerns and its horizon of meaning.

In what follows I want to elucidate some of the most important features of the *Historia Calamitatum* as a narrative text and, in so doing, indicate how narrative codes can differ from genres. Reflecting on the *Historia,* we can perceive three different though interrelated codes working in the narrative: (1) the confessional autobiography, archetypally represented in the Christian tradition by Augustine's *Confessiones;* (2) the moral allegorical interpretation of the adultery of Venus and Mars; and (3) the stereotyped Christian argument against women, that is, antifeminist discourse. These three discourses determine the text's narrative structure, but because they are not always compatible, junctures and paradoxes appear in the narrative. These impediments are multiplied by the narrator's use of prolepsis to collapse the narrative line. The narrator attempts to resolve and transform all these junctures, but the result is that the resolutions lead to new junctures and paradoxes.

Students of medieval iconography and allegory will recognize that the Venus and Mars code is closely connected with the antifeminist code. The adultery of Venus and Mars (male *virtus* corrupted by female *luxuria*) was often used as an example to bolster the argument against women. But the correlation of these two codes is short-circuited by the *Historia's* particular realization of the genre of confessional autobiography with its portrayal of the sinner redeemed by grace. Unlike autobiography, which denotes a specific narrative form, the codes of Venus and Mars and antifeminism may be figured in a variety of genres, but they are not themselves genres. The result is that the genre of the confessional autobiography links the two codes so that the instrument of sin in one code becomes the occasion for salvation in the other.

I

Like most autobiographies, especially those referred to as "literary," Abelard's *Historia* develops a tension or dialectic between the past narrated self and the present narrating self. In the Christian tradition this dialectic is often realized as the story of the sinner converted, the best known example of which is Augustine's *Confessiones.*The *Confessiones* is the principal example of a particular narrative type and is not necessarily a "source" for Abelard's text. Within the system of a literary text, we need only identify the type behind the text rather than establish a genetic relationship between texts in the same genre. Usually, but not always, changes from the past tense to the present tense define the character of the speaking "I" at any point in the narrative. Augustine narrates his historia to show how God's grace and providence can guide even the most hardened sinner to salvation. To do so, he repeatedly contrasts his former carnal, superficially verbal self with his converted self which attends to the spirit and the inner illumination of the Logos.

To cite just one example: In retrospect Augustine analyzes his former self harshly, even as his reprobate soul was turning toward heaven.

Nec inveniebam, donec amplecterer mediatorem dei et hominum, hominem Christum Iesum, qui est super omnia deus benedictus in saecula, vocantem et dicentem: ego sum via veritatis et vita, et cibum, cui capiendo invalidus eram, miscentem

carni: quoniam verbum caro factum est, ut infantiae nostrae
lactesceret sapientia tua, per quam creasti omnia. non enim tene-
bam deum meum Iesum humilis humilem, nec cuius rei magistra
esset eius infirmitas noveram. (VII.18)

[But I could not find it, until I embraced the mediator between
God and man, the man Jesus Christ, who is above all God blessed
forever, calling to me and saying, "I am the Way, the Truth, and
the Life," and who mingled in the body that food which I am
unable to take. For the Word was made flesh, so that your wisdom, by which you created all things, might nourish our infancy.
I, not humble enough, did not apprehend my Lord Jesus Christ,
who had made himself humble; nor did I yet know what his
infirmity would teach us.][4]

Throughout the *Confessiones,* the redeemed narrator judges his former
self's pride and corruption while supplying the audience with a clear
view of his present piety and learned ignorance.

Abelard constructs a similar distinction between his past self, the
prideful philosopher and seducer of Heloise, and his present narrating
self, the humbled, castrated philosopher of God who instructs the nuns
at the Paraclete in the proper celibate life. For instance, the narrator
says that as his worldly fame and prosperity increased, so did his
carnality.

Unde utriusque lectionis studio scholae nostrae vehementer multi-
plicatae, quanta mihi de pecunia lucra, quantam gloriam compara-
rent, ex fama te quoque latere non potuit. Sed quoniam prosperitas
stultos semper inflat, et mundana tranquillitas vigorem enervat
animi, et per carnales illecebras facile resolvit. (Pp. 181–82)

[Thus my school was notably increased in size through desire for
lectures on subjects of both these kinds, and the amount of finan-
cial profit as well as glory which it brought me cannot be concealed
from you, for the matter was widely talked of. But prosperity
always puffs up fools, and worldly comfort weakens the soul and
readily loosens its fiber through the carnal temptations.][5]

Even as he narrates the rise of his past self in the academic world, the
present self calls attention to his fall and the punishment for his sin.

Cum igitur totus in superbia atque luxuria laborarem, utriusque
morbi remedium divina mihi gratia licet nolenti contulit, ac primo

luxuriae, deinde superbiae; luxuriae quidem his me privando quibus hanc exercebam, superbiae vero quae mihi ex litterarum maxime scientia nascebatur, iuxta illud Apostoli: *Scientia inflat,* illius libri, quo maxime gloriabar, combustione me humiliando. (P. 182)

[And while I was laboring under my pride and lechery, God's grace provided a cure for each, though I willed it not, first for my sensuality, then for my pride; for my sensuality, by depriving me of those things whereby I practiced it, then for my pride, fostered in me by my knowledge of letters—and it is even as the Apostle said: "Knowledge puffs itself up"—by humiliating me through the burning of that in which I most gloried.]

This episode is only the most emphatic instance of a more general pattern in the *Historia.* The confessional autobiography develops out of a narrative mode which is retrospective or reflexive. Abelard the narrator repeatedly calls attention to the distinction between his present situation and previous events. Through prolepses he collapses the narrative line by indicating the outcome of a narrative sequence before it is completely narrated. For example, Abelard offers to marry Heloise after she becomes pregnant and the narrator goes on to add:

Assensit ille, et tam sua quam suorum fide et osculis, eam quam requisivi concordiam mecum iniit quo me facilius proderet. (P. 185)

[To this he (Fulbert) gladly assented, pledging his own faith and that of his kindred, and thereby became on good terms with me as I had sought of him—all so that he might the more easily betray me.]

The narrator here shifts the point of view to supply a motivation which was only revealed to him afterward. A few lines later the narrator repeats this prolepsis when Heloise refuses to marry him:

Iurabat illum nulla unquam satisfactione super hoc placari posse, sicut postmodum cognitum est. (Pp. 185–86)

[She swore that her uncle would never be appeased by such satisfaction as this, as, indeed, afterwards proved only too true.]

Similarly proleptic is the narrator's remark that Heloise was prophetic when she foretold what would happen if they married:

"Unum," inquit, "ad ultimum restat ut in perditione duorum
minor non succedat dolor quam praecessit amor." Nec in hoc
ei, sicut universus agnovit mundus, prophetiae defuit spiritus.
(P. 189)

["The sorrow," she said, "yet to come shall be no less than the
love we two have already known." Nor in this, as the world well
knows, was the spirit of prophecy lacking.]

The effect of these remarks, which characterize the narrator's retrospective voice, is to heighten the reader's awareness of the violent
outcome of the lovers' marriage and the abrupt elimination of the one
organ that a marriage is supposed to sanction. Therefore, the narrative
undercuts the marriage by noting how it was transformed into another
relationship.

In contrast to these three instances of the narrator's collapse of the
narrative line, two later distinctions between past and present reveal the
narrator's judgment on events in his life. Abelard narrates how his
enemies—Alberic, Lotulphe, and Rudolphe, archbishop of Rheims—
sought to have his writing on the Trinity condemned because he read it
in public. He then comments upon the current state of theological
writing:

Et hoc perutile futurum fidei Christianae, si exemplo mei mul-
torum similis praesumptio praeveniretur. (P. 195)

[It would be a notable blessing to the Christian faith if more
displayed a like presumption.]

Later, as Abelard draws his narrative to a close, the present situation of
the narrator becomes very explicit. Having recently escaped one assas-
sination plot by the monks at St. Gildas, Abelard calls attention to the
insecurity of his present position:

In quo etiam adhuc laboro periculo, et quotidie quasi cervici meae
gladium imminentem suspicio ut inter epulas vix respirem.
(P. 210)

[In this danger I am still involved and, as it were, see a sword
which threatens my neck so that I can scarcely draw a free breath
between one meal and the next.]

These two judgments in the present tense, strategically located in the
latter part of the *Historia,* reveal a narrator who is unlike most narrators

in confessional autobiography. The narrator in Augustine's *Confessiones,* for example, also makes judgments about his former self, but they are always fortified by the enlightened perspective of the converted Augustine. Abelard, on the other hand, while he has improved somewhat on his former prideful, secular self, nonetheless portrays himself in the present as still threatened by the same violence as in the past—castration or diocesan censure and a loss of power and control. So even though the more pious narrator constructs his history as if he were truly superior to his former self, he refrains from representing his present self as wholly integrated and redeemed.

This alteration of the typical narrative resolution in the confessional autobiography results from the interrelation of two other codes in the *Historia:* the moral interpretation of the adultery of Venus and Mars and the antifeminist argument against women. These two coded discourses act like filters in the text through which the narrative genre of confessional autobiography is particularized and its specific kind of argument developed. This does not preclude the possibility that a genre may become a coded discourse, as Maria Corti has recently suggested.[6] But, in terms of the narrative dynamics a text realizes, a genre need not be a code.

I think this distinction is more than terminological hairsplitting. A code is a kind of already organized language, prefashioned and stereotyped within the system of discourse. In this sense, then, our abstractions and generalizations about genre types can be called codes, as with the confessional autobiography genre typified by Augustine. But we only know this because of forms which are repeated often enough to be discerned as a type. However, the confessional autobiography is only one of the materials from which Abelard fashions a specific text. The result is that the *Historia* achieves a generic power different from that of any other work in the confession genre, a power which uses generic properties of the stereotyped confessional autobiography as material to be directed through the *Historia's* own particular form.

II

Abelard uses the Venus and Mars code as a matrix to situate the characters in his narrative. The eleventh and twelfth centuries witnessed an increased interest in the interpretation of Ovidian myth. Ovid's writings, including the *Ars amatoria* and *Remediae amoris,* had been copied and presumably read throughout the Carolingian period. But in the twelfth century Ovid's works became more widely disseminated and more diversely used. Accordingly, there arose a new need to rationalize what so many were already reading.[7]

During the twelfth and thirteenth centuries works such as the *Ovide moralise* codified the moral interpretations of Ovid's mythological narratives. To use Ian Ramsey's terms, the adultery of Venus and Mars was a "picture model" which was "read off"[8] as the corruption of manly virtue *(vir> virtus)* by feminine *luxuria*. This reductive interpretation was obviously motivated by antifeminist arguments, yet it provided a stable framework for evaluating human action. When joined with the Platonic–Christian duality of rest and restlessness, the *virtus-luxuria* scheme enabled Christian orthodoxy to distinguish idleness from profitable action, as well as from active meditation which could be confused with idleness. Like other Christian dualities, rest was divided into: (1) peaceful harmony associated with God and other worldly values, and (2) luxurious idleness which leads to corruption and sin. The contemplative person in the cloister, therefore, was ideally to pursue busy leisure *(negotiosissimum otium)*.[9] In both secular and sacred contexts, the Venus and Mars code produced examples of what happens when manly virtue (or redeemable mankind) fails to resist female sexual temptation. Women are stereotyped as carnal temptresses who lure men to idleness and sin, often represented allegorically as the hook baited with sex.[10]

By distributing the various elements of the Venus and Mars myth in the text, Abelard transforms his physical castration into universal terms. Historical fact becomes an example of an ideal type. He begins the *Historia* by describing himself as a Mars not on the battlefield but "in the bosom/lap of Minerva" (Minervae gremio). As the eldest son of a somewhat influential fief holder in Brittany, Abelard significantly does not think of himself as giving up knighthood, just changing the equipment and the locale.[11] He says he put on the "armor of logical reasoning" (dialecticarum rationum armaturam) and "to the prizes of victory in war . . . preferred the battle of minds in disputation" (trophaeis bellorum conflictus praetuli disputationum) (pp. 175–76). His tongue was his sword and Truth the ultimate prize. We do not have to debate the phallic implications of the sword or the tongue to see that for Abelard the virtuous combat of the cerebral Martian philosopher meant verbal dialectic.[12] Although the narrator compares himself to other figures (Ajax, Jerome, St. Anthony), these references are subsumed by the Venus and Mars code.

When Abelard narrates his seduction of Heloise, he combines the discourse of Augustinian confession with the Venus and Mars code. Intellectual success and pride, he says, go hand in hand with carnal temptations (pp. 181–82), a pattern also traced out in the *Confessiones*.

In the *Historia,* verbal action with the tongue is equated with or at least linked to sexual activity with the penis. But the correlation of pride and sexuality produces at this point in the *Historia* an inversion of the typical character of Venus in the Venus and Mars code. He describes Heloise less as a sexual temptress and more as a stereotyped object of lust. When he finds himself attracted to his pupil, Abelard must have her.

> Tanti quippe tunc nominis eram et inventutis et formae gratia praeminebam ut quamcumque feminarum nostro dignarer amore nullam vererer repulsam. (P. 183)

> [Then I was so well known, and I possessed such advantages of youth and charm, that no matter what woman I might favor with my love, I dreaded rejection of none.]

Although he mentions Heloise's learning as well as her beauty, the narrator refers to her as the "tender lamb" (agnam teneram) entrusted to the "ravenous wolf" (famelico lupo) (p. 183). This initial description of Heloise as prey is paradoxical in view of Abelard's persistent representation of himself as victim in the *Historia.* Nonetheless, it is consistent with the narrator's portrait of his proud former self.

III

Most significant about the seduction of Heloise is the way the narrator reflects on his pride that led to a fall while he recapitulates without qualification the antifeminist argument that women have always been men's ruin. Whereas the initial description of Heloise refrained from representing her as a Venus type, the antifeminist code enables that characterization to appear in the text. As Abelard's libidinal withdrawal deepens, his performance as a teacher suffers:

> Et quo me amplius haec voluptas occupaverat, minus philosophiae vacare poteram et scholis operam dare. (P. 184)

> [And the more these pleasures absorbed me, the less time I devoted to philosophy and to the work of the school.]

The narrator no longer equates sexual and verbal prowess but contrasts the two:

> Quantum autem maestitiam, quos gemitus, quae lamenta nostri

super hoc scholares assumerent, ubi videlicet hanc animi mei
occupationem, immo perturbationem, praesenserunt, non est
facile vel cogitare. (P. 184)

[As for the sorrow, the groans, the lamentations of my students
when they perceived the preoccupation, indeed the chaos, of my
mind, it is hard even to imagine them.]

From one perspective, this episode in the *Historia* inverts the stereotyped courtly love relationship in which the lover is ennobled by his
passion and is therefore a superior public performer. The Venus and
Mars code overrides that of ennobling love, so that Abelard's passion
deprives him of his verbal sword. When the lovers are discovered and
Abelard is cast out of the uncle's house, the narrator makes explicit the
code's textual control by referring specifically to the story of Venus and
Mars' capture *in flagrante delicto* (p. 184).

When Heloise suffers the punishment of so many other literary fallen
maidens who have transgressed sexually, Abelard plans to marry her
and so begs for her uncle's forgiveness:

Nec ulli mirabile id videri asserens, quicumque vim amoris exper-
tus fuisset, et qui quanta ruina summos quoque viros ab ipso
statim humani generis exordio mulieres deiecerint memoria
retineret. (P. 185)

[I pointed out that what had happened could not seem incredible
to anyone who had ever felt the power of love, or who remem-
bered how, from the very beginning of the human race, women
had cast down even the noblest men to utter ruin.]

This passage generates another paradox in the *Historia*. On the one
hand, Heloise is the stereotyped Venus–woman who ruins men with
sexual temptation. But then a few lines later she is the voice of antifeminism, telling Abelard why a philosopher should not marry and
recounting the cases against marriage made by Jerome, Seneca, and
others. Heloise's paradoxical position here seems to be motivated in
part by a form of the Eve–Virgin dualism. Abelard cannot separate
Heloise from the interpretation he uses to organize the narrative. So
Heloise is a Venus type. But her place in the conversion story defined
by the confessional autobiography demands that she also bring respect
to women through the Christian vocation. So she is also a Virgin type
and the wise woman who counsels Abelard well. Marrying her, she
says, seals the lovers' doom and sorrow (p. 189). Since Abelard figures

Heloise's character within the matrix of the Venus and Mars code, Helen voices the corollary argument from within the antifeminist code. As a result, the text attempts to redeem both the lovers, but not entirely successfully. The sexual ideology of the Venus and Mars code prevents Abelard from closing off the conversion narrative and from integrating Heloise into the norms of the narrative. Just as Heloise's uncle can only interpret Abelard as a trusted tutor who betrayed his employer, so Abelard can only interpret Heloise within a coded structuring of reality.

IV

Abelard's castration is the central episode in the *Historia*. Here again, the text absorbs historical fact in the ideal type.[13] The matrices of the Venus and Mars code and the antifeminist code transform the physical castration into a universal action. In the process, the referents and significances of the two codes are themselves transformed. For his sexual sin, Abelard is punished in the part which sinned. He justifies his castration as God's appropriate measure against his pride and carnality. He literalizes Jesus' command, when talking about fornicators, to cut off that member which offends against the whole man (Matt. 5.29-30). Abelard's castration is also part of the Venus and Mars matrix through which the confessional autobiography is filtered. His sexual mutilation corresponds to Mars' figurative unmanning by Venus–Woman–Luxury.

Abelard's use of the confessional autobiography genre enables him to vary the Venus and Mars code and to represent his castration as a loosening of the fleshly bonds which held him back from true spiritual chastity and virtue. Although he enters the monastery at first out of necessity, he comes to be a philosopher as much of God as of this world. But once he applies his intellectual talents to theology, Abelard (modeling himself on Origen) becomes a kind of Venus who uses the hook of the secular arts and the bait of learning to lure his students "ad verae philosophiae lectionem" (p. 191) (to the study of true philosophy). This inverts the usual signification of the Venus and Mars code, where Venus is often referred to as hooking the man with the bait of sex and so depriving him of power and control.

As a sign in iconographic painting, the hook reveals phallic associations which enable it to function either as an extension of the penis or as a substitute for it. The hook then becomes a symbol of control in a social structure where the male is the dominant sex. In the Fisher King motif, the impotent monarch (wounded in the thigh, castrated) fishes in the water, thereby abdicating his responsibilities to his equally sterile kingdom. Christian interpretation and iconography often exploited the image in terms of the two loves in the world: God the divine fisher, who baited his hook/cross with Christ in order to catch Satan and destroy death (Job 41.1), and Venus, God's secular counterpart, who lures men to sex, sin, and death. The image of the hook has retained some of these associations in our own time. Prostitutes are called hookers and "to fish in another man's pond" is a euphemism for adultery.

Once this basic dichotomy becomes coded, transformations and substitutions are possible. For example, the popular etymology *amicus ab hamo* (see Isidore, *Origines,* 10.5) is reversed by Andreas Capellanus to incorporate the connotations of spiritual or divine love into a text which deals essentially with male–female relationships in terms of class ideology. In Botticelli's *Venus and Mars,* the hook is replaced by the more naturalistic representation of Mar's lance. But in the painting, the lance is controlled from Venus' side of the canvas. The specific thing represented—fishhook, lance—is not as important as the connotations it signifies and the relationships it establishes. In the euphemism-proverb, "To fish in another man's pond," the castrater is not a woman but the "other man," whereas in the *Historia* and most other texts in Western Europe the semantic field of castration is mapped out primarily in male/female terms (Barthes' *S/Z* notwithstanding).

As a castrater, Abelard represents himself as a feminized, or perhaps desexualized, figure who leads students to the study of Christian philosophy through secular learning. The absent member affirms the community values and the primacy of Christian theology in the narrative. The students retrace the same path which Abelard himself took from secular to sacred philosophy. As Abelard articulates it, the intellectual conversion is a variation of the more dramatic conversion story typified by Augustine's *Confessiones* and the earlier part of the *Historia.* But the narrative transformation of the martial Abelard into a feminine Christian philosopher leads to another castration: the burning of his book on the Trinity, composed with his tongue, the sword of the philosophical Mars. Earlier, the narrator had proleptically linked his castration and the bookburning:

Luxuriae quidem his me privando quibus hanc exercebam, superbiae vero quae mihi ex litterarum maxime scientia nascebatur, iuxta illud Apostoli: *Scientia inflat,* illius libri, quo maxime gloriabar, combustione me humiliando. (P. 182)

[For my sensuality by depriving me of those things whereby I practiced it, then for my pride, fostered in me by my knowledge of letters—and it is even as the Apostle said: "Knowledge puffs itself up"—by humiliating me through the burning of that in which I most gloried.]

Later, he highlights the correspondence:

Conferebam, cum his quae in corpore passus olim fueram, quanta nunc sustinerem, et omnium hominum me aestimabam miserrimum. Parvam illam ducebam proditionem in comparatione huius iniuriae, et longe amplius famae quam corporis detrimentum plangebam. (Pp. 196–97)

[Comparing these new sufferings of my soul with those I had formerly endured in my body, it seemed that I was the most miserable among men. Indeed that earlier betrayal had become a little thing in comparison with this later evil, and I lamented the hurt to my fair name far more than the one to my body.]

In the narrative line, Abelard's seductive teaching at St. Denis and the burning of his book recapitulate his seduction of Heloise and his castration. Throughout the *Historia* the narrator represents himself as Mars unmanned, whether by a vindictive uncle or envious teachers of philosophy. Abelard's literal castration is the type which the text repeats in other forms as the violation of a virtuous man by a hostile public.

The narrative line in the *Historia* produces juncture after juncture, with each narrative resolution leading to new threats. After his book on the Trinity is burned, Abelard is hounded by various enemies. He eventually becomes the abbot of the notoriously corrupt abbey at St. Gildas while also helping to found the Paraclete for Heloise and her community. As the *Historia* comes to a close, we find that the narrative situation has actually changed very little. Abelard is still threatened by the sword at his throat (p. 210), still considers women inferior to men, and is still wary of women who have control over men (pp. 206–09).[14] However, he has cast away at least part of his Martian character, his wrathful, arrogant pride:

Quod diligenter ille sapientum sapientissimus attendebat, cum in Proverbiis diceret: *Non contristabit iustum quidquid ei acciderit.* Ex quo manifeste a iustitia eos recedere demonstrat, quicumque pro aliquo sui gravamine his irascuntur quae erga se divina dispensatione geri non dubitant. (P. 211)

[The wise man of old had this in mind when he said in his Proverbs: "No evil will befall the just." By this he clearly shows

that whosoever grows wrathful for any reason against his suffering
has therein departed from the way of the just, because he may not
doubt that these things have happened to him by divine dispen-
sation.]

Theoretically, Abelard's castrations and transformations could go on
forever in the narrative line. Once Abelard universalizes his castration
to interpret all his relationships in the world, the narrative becomes a
never ending explanation of what the narrator comprehends as victimization. The closure of the conversion story is opened out by the
narrator who reflectively judges each episode only to remain within the
interpretation of his life as victimization, a kind of uncanny circling
which generates the text. In the end, only God resolves all paradox and
narrative in his teleology and providence.

Some deconstructions of narrative unravel the threads from which
the narrative fabric is woven and so decenter the logocentric edifices
which assert the privileged position of literature or art. But I would
prefer to unravel threads to see how the whole cloth is fabricated. By
spinning out the various codes in the *Historia,* we can more adequately
account for the specific power of the kind of work it is. Part of that
power is seductive in that it reinforces the stereotyped argument against
women who destroy men's virility and virtue. The act of interpretation
provides us with a reflective position within which we may challenge
the ideological reduction of human relationships to a static equilibrium
of either/or choices. At the same time, our interest as readers of the
Historia depends primarily on our attention to the narrative consciousness which weaves together the threads of discourse into a concrete
verbal discourse which is not duplicated anywhere else. Codes and
stereotypes are the materials of literature, but they are not in themselves literature. While codes may be repeated indefinitely, the internal
generic shape of each work is a controlled nexus of conflicting languages and paradoxical codes. Heloise is and is not a sexual temptress,
Abelard is and is not a lesser man after his castration. The junctures we
have noted in the *Historia* determine the text's multivocal quality. But
the impulse of the narrative line continuously attempts to resolve those
paradoxes and junctures. So the text is located between its multivocal
structure and its univocal formal principle. The narrative in the *Historia*
is generated by the very paradoxes which it seeks to resolve. It establishes a set of verbal matrices which correlate several codes, but in
the end it is a particular narrative with its own telos.

University of Delaware

NOTES

This essay is from a larger interpretation of sexuality and narrative, in progress. Versions were presented to an NEH-funded interdisciplinary colloquium on women in the Middle Ages (1979) and a special MLA session on medieval Latin narrative (1979).

1. See Peter Dronke, *Abelard and Heloise in Medieval Testimonies* (Glasgow: University of Glasgow Press, 1976), pp. 23–24.

2. Dronke, in *Abelard and Heloise,* conveniently summarizes the history of the debate about the letters. That the letters are exemplary, and therefore not factual, has been argued most cogently by Peter von Moos, *Mittelalterforschung und Ideologiekritik: Der Gelehrtenstreit um Heloise* (Munich: Wilhelm Fink, 1974). But such arguments are misleading to the extent they presuppose that "factual" excludes "exemplary" and vice versa, especially in the Middle Ages.

3. *S/Z*, trans. Richard Miller (New York: Farrar, Straus and Giroux, 1974), pp. 20–21. Umberto Eco has provided a more technical, less metaphorical definition, but his general term is very much like Barthes' *(A Theory of Semiotics* [Bloomington: Indiana University Press, 1976], pp. 36–40).

4. *Confessiones,* ed. P. Knoll (Leipzig: Teubner, 1909). The translation is mine.

5. Page numbers in the text refer to Joseph T. Muckle's edition of the *Historia* in *Medieval Studies* 12 (1950), 163–213. Translations are adapted from Muckle's translation (Toronto: Pontifical Institute of Mediaeval Studies, 1964).

6. *An Introduction to Literary Semiotics,* trans. Margherita Bogat and Allen Mandelbaum (Bloomington: Indiana University Press, 1978), pp. 124–31.

7. See: Jean Leclercq, *The Love of Learning and the Desire for God,* trans. Catharine Misrahi (New York: Fordham University Press, 1961), pp. 139–58; Charles H. Haskins, *The Renaissance of the Twelfth Century* (Cambridge: Harvard University Press, 1955), pp. 107–09.

8. See *Religious Language* (New York: Macmillan Co., 1957) and *Models and Mystery* (New York: Oxford University Press, 1964). In a picture model the reader believes he can "read off discourse from it without let or hindrance." Ramsey considers the picture model less satisfactory in theological explanation than "disclosure models" which enable one to develop an insight into a structure of universal significance. It may be argued that in the *Historia* Abelard makes an attempt to transform his castration by switching his interpretive framework from a picture model to a disclosure model. But that attempt is singularly unsuccessful.

9. See Leclercq, *Love of Learning,* pp. 84–85.

10. For a convenient summary of these interpretations, see Earl G. Schreiber, "Venus in the Medieval Mythographic Tradition," *JEGP* 74 (1975), 519–35. Among the collections of allegorized myths most commonly used in the Middle Ages, see: Fulgentius, *Mithologiae,* ed. Rudolph Helm (Leipzig: Teubner, 1898), II.7; *'Ovide moralise.' Poeme du commencement du quatorzieme siecle,* ed. C. de Boer (1920; rpt. Wiesbaden: Martin Sandig, 1966), IV.1488–1755.

11. Cf. Georges Duby's study of the twelfth-century idea of scholar-knights; "Dans la France de Nord-Ouest au XII[e] siecle: Les 'jeunes' dans la societe aristocratique," *Annales* 19 (1964), 835–46.

12. Evelyn Birge Vitz, following Jean Jolivet, has called attention to the grammatical and sexual resonance of *copulator* in the *Historia;* "Type et individu dans 'l'autobiographie' medievale," *Poetique* 6, no. 24 (1975), 441–42. Vitz also avoids authenticity and discusses the *Historia* as autobiographical *ecriture.*

13. Professor Marcia Colish has reminded me that medieval canon law distinguished between two kinds of criminal rape: (1) violent rape against the woman's will, and (2) seduction, the use of flattery and deception to sexually control a woman, usually a minor, against the wishes of her parents or tutors. The first was punishable by death or excommunication, while the second might demand castration. See A. Bride, "Rapt," in *Dictionnaire de théologie catholique* (Paris: Librairie Letouzey et Ane, 1937).

14. This nonresolution in the text may help decide the authenticity of Letter 8 in which Abelard stipulates that men must be dominant even in the convent. It would be possible to show how all the letters attributed to Abelard and Heloise are elaborations of the principal relationships established in the *Historia*.

Carthaginian Love: Text and Supertext in the *Roman de la Rose*

John V. Fleming

*T*he long dialogue between Reason and the Lover with which Jean de Meun introduces his continuation of the *Roman de la Rose* contains also his denouement, when, with fifteen thousand lines yet to go, the two characters part company forever. Their rift, whether viewed as comic or tragic or both at once, as Jean himself seems to view it, is the inevitable outcome of their protracted and often spirited quarrel about love—the thing itself, and the words used of it. The episode is lengthy (three thousand lines) yet dense with a complexity of argument and image which no critic has so far addressed. It might be said of the *Roman* as a whole that it is a poem so foreign to us that we understand its easiest ideas only with great labor. Its real difficulties we may never even identify.

All the subjects touched upon in that lengthy dialogue are of crucial importance for the broader strategies of the whole poem, but one subject in particular, friendship, has a privileged status, pointing as it does to the major character Amis, to the meaning of the lover's compact with the God of Love, and to the more bizarre alliances of Reason and Danger, Amours and Faussemblant, the Vekke and the Lover, and so forth. Within the more limited economy of the episode itself, it is the subject of friendship which most clearly displays the distance between Reason and the Lover and thus adumbrates their definitive parting of the ways.

The *Roman de la Rose* is a poem of contexts; every part of it explains, qualifies, illuminates another part. It is therefore useful to note the general context of the argument about friendship, which in fact comes in the midst of Reason's taxonomy of *love*. Reason defines a number of different *kinds* of love, always at some length and often with copious

51

literary exemplification. Among love's genres are sexual passion (a
mental illness), natural concupiscence (an innate proclivity), and so
forth. Among the loves here defined is friendship, "mutual good will
among men, without any discord, in accordance with the benevolence
of God." This love called friendship is, according to Reason, virtuous;
and she contrasts it sharply with that love which has captured the
Lover, love *par amours.* The Lover's response to this lecture is highly
irrational—irrationality is, after all, what is signified by the dramatic
tableau of a man arguing against Reason—but also richly comic. The
beginning and the end of the argument, omitting several hundred lines
of exemplification, are as follows:

> Amistiez est nomee l'une,
> c'est bone volanté conmune
> des genz antr'els, sanz descordance
> selonc la Dieu benivolance,
> et soit entr'els conmunité
> de touz leur biens en charité,
> si que par nule entencion
> n'i puisse avoir excepcion.

> [Amant:] Ci ne finastes hui de dire
> que je doi mon seignor despire
> por ne soi quele amor sauvage.
> Qui cercheroit jusqu'an Quartage . . .
> n'avroit il pas aconseu. . . .
> Neis Tulles, qui mist grant cure
> en cerchier secrez d'escripture
> n'i pot tant son engin debatre
> qu'onc plus de .iii. pere ou de .iiii.,
> de touz les siecles trespassez
> puis que cist mond fu conpassez,
> de si fines amors trouvast.[1]

[One (of the species of love) is called friendship. It is a shared
good will between people, without discord, consistent with
the goodness of God, so that there is between them in charity
the shared possession of all their goods in such wise that on
no account may there be an exception to this arrangement. . . . (The lover responds:) All day long you haven't
stopped telling me that I ought to betray my liege-lord on behalf
of I don't know what sort of bestial love. He who would search as

far as Carthage . . . wouldn't find it. . . . Even Cicero, who took great pains in searching out the secrets of texts, was unable to tax his brain enough to find more than three or four examples of such elegant love in all the centuries since the world was created.]

That is, Reason defines friendship as a species of love which she recommends instead of the love of Amours (the Lover's *seignor,* 5346); and the Lover says, in effect, "The kind of love you are counseling—namely friendship—cannot be found on earth. I wouldn't find it even if I were to go as far as Carthage. Not even Cicero could find more than three or four such examples in the history of the world."

The passages of text are very curious, and they raise a number of problems which the poem's editors and commentators have never recognized, let alone resolved. Yet the kind of problems here raised (linguistic precision, Jean's attitude toward his sources, the nature of the classical learning of the *Roman,* the whole question of the poem's "intertextuality") are among those which offer most promise for the understanding of a work concerning which there is little common critical agreement beyond the shared perception of its crucial presence in the history of the poetry of late medieval Europe. The specific questions which the texts ask include two I shall pursue in this essay: why is friendship an *amor sauvage?* and why would the Lover not find it even were he to go to Carthage? The search for answers to those questions will involve the discovery that for Jean de Meun a "text" is sometimes a pretext and sometimes a supertext.

What I mean by the term "supertext," a neologism which I advance with embarrassment, will presently emerge, though in the most general terms I allude to the operation within a poem of a secondary literary presence of a specially, and often uniquely, privileged authority. A supertext is not a text, for it appears only by inference or implication; it is not a subtext because it does not infiltrate from below but commands from above. The concept is necessarily related to that of "intertextuality," and it has a particular vitality with regard to medieval literary culture which in many ways fostered real or feigned subservience of original genius to literary authority and encouraged complex patterns of literary dependence, appropriation, imitation, and what in our own day would be downright plagiarism.

Such problems are acutest of all, perhaps, precisely with those major figures of the vernacular period for whom the literary calling inevitably yoked translation and original composition. There were many such artists, but for representative purposes two conspicuous poet-translators immediately present themselves: Jean de Meun and Geoffrey Chaucer. These two men, whose literary careers viewed in their totality are so strikingly similar, are in one sense *always* translating an anterior text. Jean's French *Boece* is one way he "handles" the *Consolatio;* the central structural metaphor of the *Roman de la Rose* is another. Chaucer's actual translation of the *Roman* we do not have, yet we see him "translating" Jean de Meun on virtually every page he wrote. We search for canons by which we can hope to adjudicate complex literary relationships which include, in one and the same instance, deference if not servility on the one hand and an assertive competitiveness on the other.

I

In the text from the *Roman de la Rose,* which is the subject of our inquiry, there is one explicit appeal to the authority of an *auctor* outside the poem: Cicero. As it happens no classical author could be better suited to exemplify the dilemma of the Christian writer interested in the "classics," a dilemma which, in the early Christian period, created some of our surest models of the medieval supertext. Cicero presented the problem of "Christian humanism" in its acutest form, for he combined in his life and reputation unassailable literary authority and an unimpeachable moral character. He was not merely a great writer, the greatest prose stylist of all time, but a great man; and his severe stoicism so often approached the categories of Pauline righteousness that whole paragraphs and indeed essays could be appropriated in their integrity to the school books of Christian children for a thousand years. Yet it is precisely Cicero who presents the paradigm case for our discussions of the ambiguous attitude of the Fathers to the classics, an attitude traditionally illustrated in scholarly discussion by Jerome and Augustine.

Two famous set-pieces, the first in the letter to Eustochium, the other in the third book of the *Confessions,* offer apparently stark alternative Christian possibilities. Jerome, convicted by Christ himself of being a "Ciceronian," is scourged for that crime till his sobs of pain mingle with cries for pity.[2] On the other hand, Augustine is half converted by his reading of the *Hortensius,* a book "which contained an exortation to the love of wisdom. Indeed, Lord, that book changed my way of thinking and turned my prayers toward you."[3] The two anecdotes are actually not so far apart as they seem, and the one can help explain the other. Augustine says of Cicero's readers that they generally admired the chaff rather than the fruit. If that is culpable in a pagan, how much worse in a Christian. Yet such is Jerome's real crime—an educated embarrassment at the stylistic crudities of the Scriptures and a guilty preference for the polished cadences of Tully.

For the purposes of this essay it is Augustine's attitude which is of the greatest interest; yet though it be the model of a "positive" Christian response to pagan culture it is by no means free from ambiguity. It would be hard to give Cicero a greater compliment than to say that he initiated Augustine's search for wisdom, a search which as we know would end only with Christ, the eternal wisdom of the Father, but even in proffering it Augustine exhibits certain grudging and patronizing reservations. "Et usitato iam discendi ordine perueneram in librum cuiusdam Ciceronis, cuius linguam fere omnes mirantur, pectus non ita"[4] ("In the standard course of study I came to a book of a certain Cicero, whose tongue nearly all admire, but not his heart"). Testard has argued that in using the categories of "heart" and "tongue," Augustine defers to Cicero's own opposition of "wisdom" and "eloquence," a hierarchy often suggested in medieval texts by "gold" and "silver" and one easily enough included among the cliched metaphors of scriptural exegesis—spirit and letter, fruit and chaff, grain and husk.[5]

Yet it is precisely the continuity with scriptural wisdom that Augustine seeks to destroy with the odd word *pectus*. Christine Morhrmann must certainly be right in suggesting that Augustine has chosen it instead of *cor* precisely because *cor* is a privileged scriptural word with privileged scriptural associations.[6] Augustine wants to make the point that though Cicero has *philosophia*, it is not the revealed *philosophia* of Christ. And however we understand the extraordinary phrase *cuiusdam Ciceronis*, it is difficult to avoid its supercillious and patronizing overtones. We cannot believe that the source of Augustine's archness is literary vanity; he does not patronize Cicero because he thinks himself a better stylist. On the other hand, he clearly thinks he is possessed of a higher wisdom, and that, perhaps, makes him a better *writer*.

Thus it is that Christian writers of the Middle Ages could at once revere the great masters of classical antiquity and, with a logic as sincere as their respect, recognize their own inevitable superiority. Christian "Ciceronianism" is, in fact, a fairly common phenomenon of late antique literature. One particularly impressive example, the *De officiis* of St. Ambrose, has been repeatedly examined by students of the classical tradition in early Christianity but nonetheless neglected with respect to its implications for the Augustinian literary tradition.[7] There is the clearest, most explicit generative relationship between the *De officiis* of Cicero and that of Ambrose.[8] The subject of the latter work and its principal philosophical assumptions, its tripartite structure, its very title—all this and more Ambrose has taken from Tully, explicitly and, so far as one can tell, without apology or self-conscious tension. I do not mean, of course, that Ambrose's attitude toward his pagan source is uncomplicated by a certain assumption of superiority and, at times, an implicit censoriousness. Yet throughout the book Cicero is regarded with manifest respect and deference as a grave moral authority, and the authority *par excellence* on Ambrose's chosen topic, duty. The debts of philosophical substance and literary form are acknowledged cheerfully and without "anxiety" so far as one can judge, and certainly without the breast-beating, literal or metaphorical, of Jerome.

The considerable controversy surrounding the nature of Ambrose's *De officiis* has in fact been excited by the author's optimistic approbation of the main lines of Cicero's thought, so that Ambrose has been identified by some as a thoroughgoing stoic, and credited by others with a conscious and syncretistic fusion of Ciceronian and scriptural philosophy.[9] But Ambrose is a "Ciceronian" only insofar as Cicero approaches being a Christian, and the distance between Cicero and Christ is sometimes a short step and sometimes a great chasm. There can be no doubt that Cicero is the giant on whose broad shoulders Ambrose rests in his *De officiis,* but it would be rash to call Ambrose, the master of Augustine, a dwarf. A giant on the back of a giant sees not merely a little further; he sees an altogether new horizon. Cicero, however grave a moral authority, lived before the illumination of Christ and beyond the illumination of the Scriptures. Ambrose pays homage to the classical moralist on every page of his book, but he likewise corrects him, confidently, and at times sharply, from the privileged perspective of Christian revelation.

I shall limit myself to a single example, though any number could be adduced. Cicero begins his third book by evoking the busy leisure of Scipio the African, of whom it was first said that "he was never less at rest than when he was at rest."[10] His point is that Scipio turned his leisure to useful and social purpose, in reflection and internal dialogue. Ambrose in his turn ratifies the importance of *otium* and *solitudo* to the ethical man, but his attitude toward Cicero's exemplary use of Scipio is one of peeved condescension. *His* third book begins not with Scipio but with David and Solomon, models of contemplation, and what he has to say of Scipio is that "he was *not* the first to understand that he was not alone when he was alone, nor less at leisure than when he was at leisure."[11] The *first* was Moses. Ambrose's *exemplum* is implicitly truer than Cicero's because it is taken from sacred history, not the history of the earthly city. By implication the moral quality which it exemplifies— though sharing a Latin vocabulary with Cicero—is likewise of a higher order than that described by Cicero. This has nothing to do either with the comparative literary abilities of the two writers or even with their comparative moral characters. It results from the simple fact that one writer is illuminated by the grace of Christ, and the other not. In the final paragraph of his *De officiis* Ambrose summarizes his claim for the work's moral utility, which, quite independent of the possible stylistic inadequacy of the essay, is firmly established in its copiousness of scriptural *exempla*.[12]

In certain manifestations this attitude could be little more than a kind of literary self-righteousness, an uncomplicated rejection of "lies" in favor of "truth." In what might be called the Dominican attitude toward poetry in the later Middle Ages, there is a coarseness that does not stop short of philistinism, and even great poets, the Chaucer of the "Retractions" or the Jean de Meun of the "Testament," were not untouched by it. But it has another vein too, one poetically much richer, and there is a major tradition of medieval Christian poetry in which biblical self-confidence led to fruitful literary competition rather than literary suppression or censorship.

The *Psychomachia* shows one strategy for taking on Vergil, the *Divine Comedy* another. Here is poetry as serious and elevated as we shall find in the Middle Ages; yet, in differing ways, the response of Prudentius and Dante to the *Aeneid* is witty, even playful. One particular poetic tradition, in which materials from pagan mythology and Christian history are brought together in what might be called competitive collation, is especially relevant in the present context. The Bible epic of "Eupolemius" gives a good example of the technique from the high Middle Ages. "Eupolemius" structures much of his poem about parallels—Joseph and Hippolytus, the golden calf and Europa's bull, the Tower of Babel and the revolt of the giants, Noah and Deucalion, Jacob and Diomedes.[13]

The classic of this genre is an older work, dating from the first Christian millennium, the so-called *Eclogue* of Theodulus. It enjoyed a long life as a medieval school-book and, as one of the *Octo Auctores Morales,* it helped keep intact in the Renaissance the remarkably enduring marriage of elegant Latin and ascetic doctrine.[14] The eclogue is a debate between the shepherd Pseustis (falsehood) and the shepherdess Alithia (truth). Pseustis proposes examples of elegant classical mythology only to be topped every time by Alithia's examples from Bible history. The final adjudication is reserved for Phronesis, well known as a grave censor from the poems of Alain de Lille and Henry of Septimello, among others, and of course her judgment is for Alithia. The eclogue thus presents an elegant model of how a Christian poet might at once delight in classical texts and avoid the errors of seeing them as truth. The *Dialogus super auctores* makes the point write explicitly that Theodulus's intention is not to dissuade his audience from *reading* pagan poetry, but to point out its deficiencies as a model for moral imitation.[15]

II

The *De officiis* was not the only moral essay of Cicero's to which great Christian writers paid the high compliment of "Christianization" for there is a yet more magnificent example in the *De spiritali amicitia* of St. Aelred of Rievaulx. Aelred's book is one of the greatest masterpieces of twelfth-century Cistercian literature, and that perforce means one of the greatest books in medieval European literature. In it Aelred does for friendship what Ambrose did for duty; he examines a Ciceronian category from the advantage of Christian revelation, exploring, in effect, what difference Christ makes for friendship. Aelred was entirely conscious of the Ambrosian pattern he followed, and he repeatedly cites Ambrose's *De officiis.*

The *De spiritali amicitia* thus provides a splendid example of twelfth-century "Christian humanism," but its relevance for the *Roman de la Rose* is more pointed still. Jean de Meun translated the book from Latin into French, and in the famous dedicatory epistle to his *Boece* he proudly lists its title *(Espirituelle amistié)* along with other translations and the *Roman de la Rose* in the catalogue of his *oeuvre.*[16] This is in some ways a remarkable fact, but more remarkable still is the fact that scholars have not stampeded to explore a major work devoted to a subject developed at length in the *Roman de la Rose* and known to have been translated by the *Roman*'s author. This neglect is to some extent explained by the fact that no copy of the French translation is known, so that the text has not been able to force itself upon the attention of students of French literature; but I think also that the prevailingly fashionable descriptions of Jean de Meun as an "immoralist," a "bourgeois realist," a "phallicist," and a social and political revolutionary have made it seem unlikely that his poetry could be much illuminated by monkish books on monkish friendship.

Such assumptions were fruitfully challenged some years ago by Lionel Friedman, who set out to examine Reason's definition of friendship (4655 ff.) in the light of a comparative examination of relevant portions of the *De amicitia* and the *De spiritali amicitia.*[17] In analyzing this passage he concluded that "it is impossible to consider Raison's definition a 'translation' of Cicero's and difficult to believe it a paraphrase." He makes a good attempt to sort things out, but his own discussion is muddled by the fact that he cites, as Cicero's definition of friendship, that of Aelred, thus rather begging the case.[18] The mistake is understandable, for the two definitions are nearly identical, yet crucially different. We shall do well to have them before our eyes.

Cicero's definition of friendship in the *Laelius* (vi.20) is this: "Est enim amicitia nihil aliud, nisi omnium diuinarum humanarumque rerum cum beniuolentia et caritate consensio"[19] ("Friendship is nothing else than this: agreement concerning all things human and divine, with benevolence and charity"). It is this definition, in a slightly different form, that Aelred and his friend Ivo adopt, tentatively, as a kind of "working position" for their dialogue in *De spiritali amicitia* (I.11–12).

> *Aelredus:* Nonne satis tibi est hinc quod ait Tullius: *Amicitia est rerum humanarum et diuinarum cum beneuolentia et caritate consensio?*
>
> *Ivo:* Si tibi sufficit ista diffinitio, mihi iudico satisfactum esse.[20]

> [*Aelred:* Is not what Tully says sufficient for you: "Friendship is agreement concerning things human and divine, with benevolence and charity?"
>
> *Ivo:* If this definition suffices for you, I reckon it is satisfactory for me.]

It does suffice, but only for a moment; for when Aelred next cites it, it has enjoyed a crucial increment. In the first place he insinuates the definition into the midst of a scriptural quotation (Acts 4.32) which identifies friendship with the apostolic communism of the church at Jerusalem. Of the early Christians he then says (I.29), "Quomodo non inter eos *rerum diuinarum et humanarum cum caritate et beneuolentia* fuit summa *consensio,* quibus erat *cor unum et anima una?*"[21] ("How could there not be amongst them total *agreement concerning things human and divine, with benevolence and charity,* for whom *there was one heart and one spirit?*"). It is the *summa,* awarded by Friedman to Cicero, which is in fact the insight of Aelred; and it is the kind of superlative which can indicate the presence of a supertext. Basil Pennington observes that "Aelred is here repeating the definition of Cicero, adding however the significant adjective 'complete'."[22] The two definitions are not very different, merely definitively different.

Now a close textual analysis will make it obvious that Reason's definition does not come from the *Laelius* but from the *De spiritali amicitia.* It is Ciceronian only insofar as Aelred is Ciceronian, and that is so far and no further. His definition of friendship is a kind of *reductio Ciceronis ad sacram paginam,* for in it Cicero has been captured and purified by the Acts of the Apostles. Lines 4659–60 (et soit entr'els conmunite / de touz leur biens en charite [so that there is between them in charity the shared possession of all their goods]) have no basis at all in Cicero; but they are a clear echo of Acts 4.32, "Neither did any one say that aught of the things which he possessed was his own; but all things were common unto them."

Aelred's *De spiritali amicitia* was a famous book in its day, and we have long known that it was one of a select group of "humanist" texts translated by Jean de Meun. Under these circumstances we may be moved to inquire why successive editors and critics of the *Roman* have attributed Reason's concept of friendship to Cicero when it is in fact that of Aelred of Rievaulx.[23] There are several possible answers to this question, but one of them must surely be that readers of the poem have been misled by one of the strategies by which Jean de Meun hoped most wittily to signal his ironic intentions. We are misled because both Reason and Amant himself mention Cicero by name.

Shortly after defining friendship, Reason adduces a passage from Cicero's *De amicitia* in her exemplification of the theme: so says Tully *in one of his books.* This vagueness (dist Tulles en un suen distie, 4718 [says Tully in one of his writings]) is a lovely Augustinian touch, almost as good as *cuiusdam Ciceronis.* The implication is that she is not intimately familiar with his work: her *primary* source is Aelred. But this is mere *jeu d'esprit.* The truly false *cicerone* is the Lover himself who, although he affects not to know what friendship is beyond the name for some category of uncouth love, is nevertheless certain that it is impossible to find, an opinion which he rests squarely in the authority of Cicero:

> Neis Tulles, qui mist grant cure
> en cerchier secrez d'escripture,
> n'i pot tant son engin debatre
> qu'onc plus de .iii. pere ou de .iiii.,
> de touz les siecles trespassez,
> de si fines amors trouvast.
> Si croi que mains en esprouvast
> de cels qui a son tens vivoient,
> qui si ami de boiche estoient;
> n'encor n'ai ge nul leu leu
> qu'il onc en ait nul tel eu.
> Et sui ge plus sage que Tulles?

Bien seroie fols et entulles,
se tex amors voloie querre,
puis qu'il n'en a mes nule en terre.

(5375-90)

[Even Cicero, who took great pains in searching out the secrets of texts, was unable to tax his brain enough to find more than three or four examples of such elegant love in all the centuries since the world was created. I imagine that he encountered less of it among those who lived at his time and were his dinner-mates. I have never yet read anywhere that he had any such friend. And am I wiser than Tully? I should be a great fool and a madman if I wished to search for such a love, for there is none more on earth.]

Now that indeed *is* Tully who, near the beginning of his essay, reports with a sigh that one can scarcely find in all of history "three or four pairs of friends."[24]

This pessimism that so devastates the Lover is perhaps appropriate for a pagan; those who live without Christ can hardly know what friendship is, since Christ is its beginning and its end.[25] As an argument in the age of grace, however, it is feeble indeed. Aelred cited this same Ciceronian text long before the Lover ever laid eyes on his rose garden, and he rejected it as risible.

Ivo: As Tullius says, "In so many past ages, tradition extols scarcely three of four pairs of friends." But if in our day, that is, in this age of Christianity, friends are so few, it seems to me that I am exerting myself uselessly in striving after this virtue which I, terrified by its admirable sublimity, now almost despair of ever acquiring.

Aelred: It is no wonder, then, that pursuers of true virtue were rare among the pagans since they did not know the Lord, the Dispenser of virtue, of whom it is written: "The Lord of hosts, he is the King of glory." Of those who had faith in him I will give you indeed not three or four but a thousand pairs of friends, who (though the pagans take the example of Pylades and Orestes as a great marvel) were ready to die for one another.[26]

A catalogue of the ironies in Amant's response to Reason would be a long one with his talk of searching out the secrets of texts and the circumstances under which he would be a stupid fool. But the central and great irony is the folly of his appeal to moral teachings of antique pagans successfully and definitively refuted by the living experiences of Christians. *Et sui ge plus sage que Tulles?* (And am I wiser than Tully?) No, alas, but you damn well should be. To cite Cicero and ignore Aelred, whose book manifestly controls this narrative moment of the poem, is a species of pagan folly toward which neither Jean de Meun nor the audience for whom he wrote both the *Roman de la Rose* and the *Espirituelle amistié* could conceivably have taken an indulgent attitude. Nor, incidentally, could Cicero himself. Amant's desire has nothing at all to do with a *consensio* in benevolence and charity but with a *copulatio* in hypocrisy and concupiscence. *That* is the sort of friendship Cicero thought was *sauvage.*[27]

III

In analyzing our passage from the *Roman de la Rose,* we have identified one controlling text and one amusing pretext, the *De spiritali amicitia* and the *Laelius,* but neither of them will tell us why the Lover will not find *amor sauvage* in Carthage or why it would occur to him not to look for it there in the first place. To understand that we must identify yet another book hidden in the lines like a spirit present everywhere and visible nowhere, the supertext which actually commands Jean's use of Cicero and Aelred alike. Jean de Meun's supertext is the *Confessions* of St. Augustine.

The suggestion of an Augustinian "source" for an important part of the *Roman,* though it is the poem's inexorable implication, must face the opposition of tradition. E. Langlois, who wrote an important book on *Les origines et sources du Roman de la Rose,* limited Augustine's influence on the poem to a few phrases from one of his lesser books, the *De opere monachorum.*[28] Even these phrases came to Jean's attention indirectly through the polemics of William of Saint-Amour.

I myself have never shared the view that Augustine has exercised only a marginal influence on Jean's poem and, indeed, have elsewhere argued at length that the general burden of sexual doctrine in the *Roman de la Rose* reflects commonplace Augustinian statements, and especially those found in the fourteenth book of the *City of God.*[29] The present suggestion is a new one, though there is, a priori, hardly anything extraordinary in the possibility that Jean de Meun, a poet who mined for his own vernacular purposes classics from the Latin repertory of medieval letters like the *Consolation of Philosophy* of Boethius or the *Complaint of Nature* of Alain de Lille, could also have mined the

Confessions, a work which as Pierre Courcelle has shown proved almost inexhaustibly fecund to later medieval writers. But since what goes without saying too often goes unsaid I might make the explicit point that there is an overarching generic kinship between the *Confessions* and the *Roman de la Rose* which all the differences between the two works, however marked, cannot compromise. This kinship is reflected both in theme and in structure.

The great theme of both works is, of course, love. Guillaume de Lorris, in the proem to the romance, claims that he will expose nothing less than the whole Art of Love:

> ce est li *Romanz de la Rose,*
> ou l'art d'Amors est tote enclose. (37–38)

> [This is the *Romance of the Rose,*
> in which the whole Art of Love is contained.]

There is throughout the *Roman* an urgency about love which, however carefully circumscribed, is always intense and often does not stop short of the comic. Whether in the practices of mental eroticism taught by the God of Love in Guillaume's part of the poem or in the altogether more robust sexuality of Jean's denouement, we see the Lover in the grip of a power which will not be denied, over which he has no control, and toward which the only appropriate posture is that of submission. This phenomenon has been universally remarked but diversely explained by the poem's critics, usually in terms of such concepts as "courtly love" and "naturalism."

I do not intend in this brief essay to enter into an extended discussion of the question, though I do want to point out that the poetic situation of the *Roman* is entirely consistent with Augustinian teaching. Love is, for Augustine, inexorable, the absolutely fundamental fact of what has come to be called his "anthropology." He can imagine a human life without love no more than he can imagine human life without food. Man was born for love, will have it, must have it. Man's viciousness, but also his promise of glory, are tied to a desperate and abandoned quest for love. Love is, indeed, man's destiny. "Thou has made us for thyself," he writes in the justly famous opening paragraph of the *Confessions,*"and our heart is restless until it finds its rest in Thee." Moral analysis in Augustine does not depend upon the *fact* of love, which is assumed, but on the *object* of love, a determination of reasonable volition. And this I have argued, by no means alone, is likewise the moral presupposition of the authors of the *Roman de la Rose.*

As there is basic congruence of theme between the two works, so also are there important parallels of form and structure. The *Roman de la Rose* is an extended erotic autobiography in which the first-person voice of the narrator is sounded with considerable artistic skill and artistic tact. The fictional—or if that be too controversial a word, the self-consciously artistic—use of the first-person voice in the *Confessions* is now widely recognized.[30] I am convinced, indeed, that it is the *Confessions* which provided the Middle Ages with its aptest model of vivid, exemplary fiction as we find it in such diverse works as the *Divine Comedy,* the *Canterbury Tales,* or the *Libro de buen amor.* This comes tolerably close to saying that in some sense St. Augustine's *Confessions* enabled most of what is best in medieval "moral fiction." So far as the *Roman de la Rose* is concerned, there are other, more specific parallels, as for example the structural metaphor of pilgrimage.

This is, I hope, bearable speculation, but it is speculation nonetheless. Of the positive relationships between Augustine's *Confessions* and Aelred of Rievaulx on the other hand we have abundant and conclusive proof. "His reading was in edifying books whose words are wont to bring tears," writes his biographer, "and in particular he generally had in his hands the *Confessions* of Augustine, for it was these which had been his guide when he was converted from the world."[31] What was generally in his hands was always in his heart, and his heart poured forth its fullness into the pages of the *De spiritali amicitia.*

There is not room in this brief essay to survey the extent of Aelred's debt to the *Confessions.* The first sentence of his prologue explicitly states the Augustinian theme of his work ("When I was just a lad at school . . . nothing seemed to me more sweet, nothing more agreeable, nothing more practical, than to be loved and to love") and the debt increases with every succeeding paragraph. The debt is of three sorts. There are in the first place innumerable direct citations and verbal echoes of the so much a part of Aelred's mind that they are an inevitable part of his writing. "The easy and almost unconscious reliance on the Scriptures and the reminiscences of the *Confessions* of St. Augustine and the devotional writings of John of Fecamp, derive from deep personal meditation nourished by the *lectio.*"[32] Next, Aelred is thoroughly and explicitly Augustinian in his doctrine of love, as he is indeed in all his works and most conspicuously in the stunning *De speculo caritatis,* his most extended treatment of the subject. Aelred regards friendship as a species of love, and we recall that the discussion of it in the *Roman de la Rose* follows Reason's similar definition: "Amors sunt de pluseurs manieres. . . . Amistiez est nomee l'une" (4650, 4655) ("There are several kinds of love. . . . One is called friendship"). In itself such a taxonomy would be a mere medieval commonplace, but Aelred goes much further; for he unmistakably identifies his own conception of friendship with Augustine's search for love in the *Confessions.* At the appearance of Gratian, one of the *personae* in Aelred's dialogue, Walter thus identifies him: "Here comes our friend Gratian . . . I might rightly call him friendship's child for he spends all his energy in seeking to be loved and to love."[33]

The third point, most immediately relevant to the argument of my essay, is this: Aelred adopts a quite self-consciously Augustinian attitude toward Cicero. That Cicero is the "source" of Aelred's treatise there is, from its very first page, no doubt whatsoever. There is not in the two books called *De amicitia* the same structural imitation that exists between the two books called *De officiis,* but when we move from form to content, Cicero's mind and matter are decisive. In the prologue to *De spiritali amicitia,* Aelred paints a brief history of his adolescence on top of the clear design of the master. "I was drawn now here, now there, and not knowing the law of true friendship, I was often deceived by its mere semblance. At length there came to my hands the treatise which Tullius wrote on friendship, and it immediately appealed to me as being useful because of the depth of his teaching and the gracefulness of its style."[34] The terms *gravitas sententiarum* and *suavitas eloquentiae* are obvious reflexes of Augustine's *pectus* and *lingua.* The young Aelred, like the young Augustine, was attracted to Cicero both by his eloquent style and his weighty matter.

Two or three sentences more trace the history of his conversion from the world—a journey for which his guide was Augustine's *Confessions,* as we have already heard in the testimony of his friend Walter Daniel— and his entry into the cloister. It was a pilgrimage of a few short years, recounted in perhaps two hundred words, yet how far it took him from the "world," and from Cicero. "From that time on Sacred Scripture became more attractive and the little learning which I had acquired in the world grew insipid in comparison. The ideas I had gathered from Cicero's treatise on friendship kept recurring to my mind, and I was astonished that they no longer had for me their wonted savor. For now nothing which had not been sweetened by the honey of the most sweet name of Jesus, nothing which had not been seasoned with the salt of Sacred Scripture, drew my affection so entirely to itself. Pondering over these thoughts again and again, I began to ask myself whether they could perhaps have some support from Scripture."[35]

This is a perfect paradigm of Augustinian Ciceronianism and, more generally, of "Christian humanism," the impulse to redeem the wisdom and eloquence of ancient writers who had themselves lived without the knowledge of the source of all redemption. Aelred knows exactly whose track he follows, and he sees in the intellectual career of Augustine a useful parallel to his own enterprise of "Christianizing" the moral philosophy of a pagan. Augustine's guide at the beginning of his search for truth had been none other than the ancient Tully, whose *Hortensius,* much admired by the college professors for its rhetorical flourishes, in fact contained an invitation to wisdom. A beginning is not an end; and the search that began with Cicero could end only with the God of Abraham, and Isaac, and Jacob, and the God made man, Jesus Christ. All this Aelred saw in the *Confessions,* so that when he came to write of friendship he began with Christ that he might understand Cicero.

Jean de Meun knew the *De spiritali amicitia* intimately, as perhaps only a skilled translator can, and while we have no external evidence that demonstrates the chronological relationship between the *Roman* and the *Espirituelle amistié,* Jean's very sophisticated use of Aelred's text in his poem does argue prior knowledge of the latter. Jean's reliance on Aelred can only in part be explained by his eclectic search for learned and authoritative "matter," for he found in Aelred not merely elegant wisdom on a given topic but a shared vision of the literary enterprise. Jean wished to write about friendship, and the *De spiritali amicitia* did indeed offer wonderful teaching about it; but for Jean de Meun the artist it taught a far greater lesson as well, for it provided a model, one might say *the* model, of what a work of "Christian humanism" might be.

In its pages the ancient wisdom of the pagan Cicero lives on intact in all its clarity and power, yet wonderfully increased, the teaching graced by that revelation denied to the teacher. This does not mean, of course, that the difference between the *De amicitia* and the *De spiritali amicitia* is trivial. Christian friendship is to Ciceronian friendship as Christ is to Cicero. If this comparison seems too bizarre we may wish to think of one which, while actually stranger, we have learned to accept, that of Beatrice and Vergil. The Christian concept of friendship does not *destroy* Cicero's concept; it fulfills, perfects it. Aelred began the *De spiritali amicitia* with the following sentence: "Here we are, you and I, and I hope a third, Christ, is in our midst." The presence of Christ transforms friendship, just as his presence has transformed history.

We can now return to Jean's poor Lover, for we are in a position to assess his despair at ever finding friendship. Amant himself has misled us to Cicero, but though editors and critics dally there Jean has set our path straight again and taken us to Aelred. Aelred, for his part, takes us back to Augustine. This is a complicated route, perhaps even a tortuous one; but the *Roman de la Rose* is a complex and difficult poem.

> Ci ne finastes hui de dire
> que je doi mon seignor despire
> por ne soi quele amor sauvage.
> Qui cercheroit jusqu'an Quartage . . .
> n'avroit il pas aconseü.

> [All day long you haven't stopped telling me
> that I ought to betray my liege-lord on behalf
> of I don't know what sort of bestial love.
> He who would search as far as Carthage . . .
> wouldn't find it.]

The task is an impossible one. *Amitiez,* this *ne sai quel amor sauvage,* couldn't be found even in Carthage. Now if the Lover were a rational man and not a fool, and if he were conscious of those arts of poetic indirection which he explicitly contemns, he too might have followed *amicitia*'s traces back to the *Confessions* of St. Augustine. There, at the beginning of the third book, he would have found a youth very much like himself, in love with love, in the throes of a search for an object of his love, a confused lover who mistook a hollow courtliness for virtue, and lubricity for friendship. The scene of that desperate search: Carthage, of course. "To Carthage I came, where there sang all around me in my ears a cauldron of unholy loves."[36]

Augustine identifies the fundamental carnality of his search for love in Carthage with a bold play on words, a rhyme in fact, though one shallowly concealed by the oblique case of one of its members. "Veni *Carthaginem,* et circumstrepebat me undique *sartago* flagitiosorum a morum" ("To Carthage I came, where there sang all around me in my ears a cauldron of unholy loves"). I admire Pusey's old rendition of this last phrase, "a cauldron of unholy loves"; but the more accurate rendition of *sartago* is "frying pan." *Cartago/sartago:* Carthage, a frying pan of lusts: *Carthage/sauvage.* Carthage was to be the setting of Augustine's desperate infatuation with love itself, his confused immersion in the flesh; so of course Carthage is the city in which Jean de Meun's willful and confused lover says he would never find that love which Reason calls good. Jean demands that we read his poem very carefully. Here, in a single topographic noun, is the only "textual" evidence of his supertext.

Augustine gave to Carthaginian love a definitive literary expression and a definitive moral meaning, but that love itself he did not invent. Jean de Meun, whom we must surely by now credit with a deeply sensitive appreciation of poetic contexts, has of course seen that what spiritual friendship does to the greatest writer of pagan prose Carthaginian love does to the greatest writer of pagan poetry. Several scholars, but in particular John O'Meara, have sought to identify definite patterns of artistic self-consciousness in the construction of the *Confessions*.[37] O'Meara has shown that Augustine is engaged in a clandestine literary competition with no less a rival than the great Vergil himself, and he has sketched the careful, sustained, indeed the almost schematic parallels by which Augustine has collated the experience of his own epic journey from darkness to grace with the epic journey of the *Aeneid*. These two journeys met most happily in the Latin word *errores,* the wanderings of the young Aeneas and the delusions of the young Augustine, the word which the author of the *Confessions* would use to denote both.

But the wanderers themselves met also in a particular geographical location, the city of Carthage. There Aeneas had dallied in Dido's arms while destiny languished. Augustine, who as a lad had lived beneath the shadow of those ramparts from which the distracted Dido searched the empty port for her lover, was in his own time to have a similar experience there. We know from several passages in the *Confessions,* among them some of the most moving in the book, the powerful impact which Vergil's Carthaginian episodes had upon the young Augustine, and how, when he came to write of his own triumph over the slavery of sexual passion, he alluded naturally, almost inevitably, to Aeneas's flight from Carthage.

Cartage is, then, a witty stroke, but perhaps not so witty as the word *sauvage,* which stands to the French *Cartage* as *sartago* stood to *Cartago.* *Sauvage* is the French reflex of the Latin *salvaticus,* and it can mean, in recorded medieval French examples, wild, rustic, bestial, and primitive. All these meanings inform Jean's use of the word, which defies translation. Dahlberg, in his excellent English version, chooses "bestial love," and that is of course correct. The French translator Lanly glosses the word as "un amour des premiers ages du monde"; that is also correct.[38]

The Lover no doubt intends the pejorative force of Dahlberg's "bestial." The *amor sauvage* recommended by Reason, like her frank French terms for the sexual organs, is just too outré and uncouth for words in its inconvenience for the Lover's program of seduction. But any reader of Aelred (or Aelred's teacher Augustine) will agree with

Lanly's gloss as well; _amor sauvage_ belongs to the province of social archaeology. _Amor sauvage_ is Christian friendship, and Aelred's clear teaching (I.51 ff.) is that honest friendship is the faint vestige in the postlapsarian world of that natural charity which characterized human nature "in the first ages of the world" before the Fall.[39]

In saying that he knows nothing of _amor sauvage_, the Lover is saying no more and no less than that he knows nothing of _caritas_. We insult Jean and his poem if we maintain that he seriously commends to us as a model of "belief to be transferred into action" this Lover who knows nothing of charity and willfully rejects the promptings of Reason which would teach him its rudiments. There is a fine irony in the fact that what the Lover calls bestial love is what Aelred calls friendship, and that what the God of Love teaches the Lover is what Aelred calls a "bestial impulse." "Longing undirected by reason is a bestial impulse, inclined to all illicit things, indeed unable to distinguish between licit and illicit."[40]

The great men of the Christian Middle Ages, the governors, churchmen, lawyers, and poets who made the greatest contributions of medieval cultural and intellectual life, knew that they had much to learn from the great writers of pagan antiquity, and for the most part they turned to their ancient masters with a respectful eagerness. First of all they sought tutelage in the skills of literacy, both in the Latin language and in the modes of writing well and speaking well in it, but they also gladly sat at the feet of ancient authorities on law, warfare, medicine, history, agriculture, architecture, and a hundred arts and sciences useful to the nourishment of their spiritual and material lives.

On one subject, however, they would have thought it madness to seek authoritative instruction from pagans, and that was on the subject at the very heart of their expressed social aspirations, the subject of Christian love. The pagans had nothing to teach about it, for they knew not what it was. As Ivo says to Aelred in the _De spiritali amiictia_, quite without disingenuousness, "I dó not see what the pagan (Cicero) meant by the words 'charity' or 'benevolence'."[41] Christians did, of course, know what pagan love was, both from old books and from their own lives. The sexual norms and conventions appropriate for pagans, as readers found them in the pages of Vergil and Ovid, clearly spoke to the felt experience of medieval people, but the voice was that of moral admonition, not of historical envy: "Lo here, of payens corsed olde rites."

One final point about _amor sauvage_ can bring us back to the supertext responsible at once for the complexity of these lines in the _Roman de la Rose_ and for their satisfactory explication. _Amor sauvage_ would mean "bestial love" to the Lover, and to Augustine primitive love, "a love from the first ages of the world." Surely they would find common ground in yet another implication of the term: rustic, simple, uncourtly love. That the Lover considers it dreadfully unsophisticated, coming fresh as he does from the fancy finishing school of his "lord" Cupid, is clear both from the whole tone of the context of our lines and from the marvelously apt term *fines amours* he uses for the legendary friendships of the ancients. There is good reason to think that neither Augustine nor Aelred would cavil at this imputation of rusticity.

The kind of elegance and urbanity which characterize the operation of the god Amours, the Lover's master in the *Roman,* is flatly inconsistent with moral virtue. Augustine makes this point in the same passage at the beginning of the third book. "To love then, and to be beloved, was sweet to me; but much more, when I obtained to enjoy the person whom I loved. I defiled, therefore, the spring of friendship with the filth of concupiscence, and I beclouded its brightness with the hell of lustfulness; and thus, foul and unseemly, I would fain, through exceeding vanity, be fine and courtly." The phrase here rendered "fine and courtly" is *elegans et urbanus,* and it provides, perhaps, a classical source for our Procrustean concept of "courtly love" frequently invoked to explain the amatory mysteries of medieval poems, the *Roman de la Rose* conspicuous among them. I suggest that another concept might be more useful still: Carthaginian love.

Princeton University

NOTES

1. *Le Roman de la Rose,* ed. Felix Lecoy (Paris: Champion, 1963–1970), vol. I, lines 4655–62, 5345–48, 5356, 5375–81; *The Romance of the Rose,* trans. Charles Dahlberg (Princeton: Princeton University Press, 1971), pp. 100, 110–11. These editions are cited throughout this paper.

2. *Epistola xxii (Ad Eustochium)* 30; Saint Jerome, *Lettres,* ed. J. Labourt (Paris: Belles Lettres, 1949), 144–45.

3. *Confessionum libri xiii,* ed. M. Skutella (Stuttgart: Teubner, 1969), III.iv.7; p. 41. This is the text used throughout this paper. English translations are my own, closely following those of Pusey and Watts, and the French translation of Labriolle.

4. Ibid., pp. 40–41.

5. Maurice Testard, *Saint Augustin et Ciceron* (Paris: Etudes Augustin iennes, 1958), vol. I, pp. 18 ff. For "silver and gold," see Hans–Jorg Spitz, *Die Metaphorik des geistigen Schriftsinns* (Munich: W. Fink, 1972), pp. 191 ff.

6. *Vigiliae christianae,* 30 (1959), 239.

7. But see Testard, *Augustin et Ciceron,* I, 119–20.

8. *De officiis libri tres,* ed. G. Banterle [*Sancti Ambrosi Episcopi Opera,* xiii] (Milan and

Rome: Biblioteca ambrosiana / Citta nuova, 1977), pp. 369 ff. lists the parallel readings.

9. See the excellent review of scholarship in Goulven Madec, *S. Ambrose et la philosophie* (Paris: Etudes Augustiniennes, 1978), pp. 161 ff. The most helpful single study is still R. Thamin, *Saint Ambrose et la morale chretienne au iv[e] siecle* (Paris: G. Masson, 1895).

10. *De officiis*, ed. P. Fedeli (Turin: A. Mondadori, 1965), p. 153: "nunquam se minus otiosum esse, quam cum otiosus."

11. *De officiis* III.i.1-2; Banterle, p. 274.

12. *De officiis* III.xxii.139; Banterle, p. 358. Cf. Madec, *Ambrose et la philosophie,* p. 163n.

13. Eupolemius, *Das Bibelgedicht,* ed. K. Manitius (Weimar: H. Böhlaus, 1973) p. 19; for further examples see M. Manitius, "Mittelalterliche Umdeutung antiker Sagenstoffe," *Zeits. f. vergl. Lit.* 15 (1904), 151-58.

14. *Theoduli eclogam,* ed. J. Osternacher, *Jahresbericht des bischoflichen Privat-Gymnasiums am Kollegium Petrinum in Urfahr,* vol. V (1902). The more recent edition by Huygens, with the complete commentary of Bernard of Utrecht, has been unavailable to me. On the *Octo Auctores,* see Robert Bultot, "La *Chartula* et l'enseignement du mepris du monde dans les écoles et les universités medievales," *Studi medievali* 3 (1967), 787-834.

15. "Intentio eius est sacrae paginae veritatem commendare et fabularum commenta dissuadere, non quidem ut non legantur, sed ne lectae credantur vel in actum transferantur." *Accessus ad Auctores,* ed. R. B. C. Huygens (Leiden: Brill, 1970), p. 94.

16. "Boethius' *De Consolatione* by Jean de Meun," ed. V. L. Dedeck-Hery, *Mediaeval Studies* 14 (1952), 168.

17. Lionel J. Friedman, "Jean de Meun and Ethelred of Rievaulx," *L'Esprit createur* 2 (1962), 135-41.

18. Ibid., p. 136.

19. Ciceron, *L'Amitie,* ed. L. Laurand (Paris: Belles Lettres, 1965), VI.20; p. 13.

20. *De spiritali amicitia,* ed. A. Hoste, in *Aelredi Rievallensis Opera Omnia,* Corpus Christianorum Continuatio Mediaevalis, i (Turnholt, 1972), p. 291. All citations are from this edition.

21. See the interpretation of Klaus Gunther Just, *Die Trauerspiele Lohensteins* (Berlin: Erich Schmidt, 1961), pp. 155-61, challenged by Gerald Gillespie, *Lohenstein's Historical Tragedies* (Columbus: Ohio State University Press, 1965), pp. 81-110.

22. Aelred of Rievaulx, *Spiritual Friendship,* trans. M. E. Laker (Washington: Cistercian Publications, 1974), p. 57n. The notes for this translation, from which my own renderings differ somewhat, are by Fr. Pennington.

23. Naive readers of this passage include, among others, editors Ernest Langlois and Felix Lecoy, the translator Andre Lanly, and, most recently, the critics Marc-Rene Jung, "Jean de Meun et l'allegorie," *Cahiers de l'Association internationale des etudes francaises* 28 (1976), 34-35, and John M. Fyler, *Chaucer and Ovid* (New Haven: Yale University Press, 1979), pp. 178-79.

24. *L'Amitie* IV.15; Laurand, p. 11.

25. "Constat enim Tullium uerae amicitiae ignorasse uirtutem; cum eius principium finemque, Christum uidelicet, penitus ignorauerit." *De spiritali amicitia* I.8; ed. Hoste, p. 290.

26. *De spiritali amicitia* I.25.27-28; trans. Laker, pp. 56-67.

27. *L'Amitie* XXI.79-81; ed. Laurand, pp. 42-43.

28. Ernest Langlois, *Les Origines et Sources du Roman de la Rose* (Paris: E. Thorin, 1891), p. 133.

29. *The Roman de la Rose, a Study in Allegory and Iconography* (Princeton: Princeton University Press, 1969).

30. See Eugene Vance, "Augustine's *Confessions* and the Grammar of Selfhood," *Genre* 6 (1973), 1-28, and Charles Dahlberg, "First Person and Personification in the *Roman de la Rose*," *Mediaevalia* 3 (1977), 37-58.

31. *The Life of Aelred of Rievaulx by Walter Daniel*, ed. F. M. Powicke (London: Nelson, 1950), p. 50.

32. Ibid., p. lxvii.

33. *Spiritual Friendship*, p. 73.

34. Ibid., pp. 45-46.

35. Ibid., pp. 46-47.

36. Augustine, *Confessions* III.i.

37. Two essays by O'Meara are particularly important: "Augustine the Artist and the *Aeneid*," *Melanges offerts a Mademoiselle Christine Mohrmann* (Utrecht and Antwerp: Spectrum, 1963), pp. 252-261; and "Virgil and Augustine: the Roman Background to Christian Sexuality," *Augustinus* 13 (1968), 307-26.

38. *Le Roman de la Rose*, trans. Andre Lanly (Paris: Champion, 1973), vol. II, p. 174.

39. Friedman, "Jean de Meun and Ethelred," p. 141.

40. II.57; Hoste, p. 313; *Spiritual Friendship*, p. 83.

41. I.14; Hoste, p. 291; *Spiritual Friendship*, p. 54.

Anatomy as Science

Devon Leigh Hodges

*I*t is commonly held that the publication of Sir Francis Bacon's *The Proficience and Advancement of Learning* in 1605 marks the end of the Renaissance and the beginning of our modern scientific world. Bacon would undoubtedly be pleased with this appraisal of his work for he too believed that he was the inaugurator of a new era. His confidence in the novelty and value of his enterprise, the construction of a "true model of the world," is everywhere apparent, but never more so than in those works in which he talks to his fictional audience, the "sons of science." With the "sons" he does not mince his words: "I suppose that I have established forever a true and lawful marriage between the empirical and the rational faculty, the unkind and ill-starred divorce of which has thrown into confusion the affairs of the human family" (*Works,* I, 246).[1] Bacon's claims for himself are claims for his anatomizing method.

For Bacon, the metaphor of anatomy, not the more familiar one of the telescope, establishes a new "natural" relationship between man, language, and nature. His assured placement of an anatomical method and language within the order of truth and nature gave authority to the discipline of science and to himself as a founding father: "no man quite escapes his presence in the haunted building of science, or the whispers of his approbation or unease."[2] This voice still murmuring in the byways of science persistently adopts fragmenting modes of articulation— induction, antithesis, aphorisms, scientific tables—that apparently have the power to open up the world to the eyes of man. But by scrutinizing Bacon's praxis, we shall see that this alleged mastery of nature by science is yet another "idol" or "false apparition." Bacon's science remains wedded to language.

Earlier anatomists, such as John Lyly, Phillip Stubbes, and Thomas Nashe, dissected the corrupt body of the world so that men could see the errors of their ways and reform their lives. Nashe, for example, conducts an anatomy of absurdity "that each one at first sight may eschew it as infectious, to shew it to the worlde that all men may shunne it."[3] Bacon is said to be a harbinger of modernity because he puts the empirical technique of anatomizing to the work of investigating the material rather than the moral condition of the world. This change in the intention of the anatomist seems at first to be the result of a new view of the proper ends of knowledge. Bacon insists that the goal of his method is the discovery of the material components of nature, not its final cause, but he also claims that the discovery of the "Forms of things" is the key to interpreting the Book of Nature and hence grounds his method in the old theological idea of nature as a book in which can be read the ultimate purpose of things.[4]

The complexity of Bacon's effort to establish the teleology of science is visible in a passage from the *Novum Organum* in which he announces his intention to conduct an "anatomy of the world." Its logic is compressed; apparently contradictory assertions are placed together as if there were no discontinuity between them. This stylistic feature makes the passage difficult to read but enables Bacon to attach his scientific project to a theological tradition, and, almost simultaneously, to attack that tradition. In this double movement the discourse of science acquires a metaphysical foundation and displaces traditional "philosophic systems" that formerly articulated the pathway toward truth. Here is the passage that concerns us:

> Again, it will be thought, no doubt, that the goal and mark of knowledge which I myself set up (the very point at which I object to in others) is not the true or the best; for that the contemplation of truth is a thing worthier and loftier than all utility and magnitude of works; and that this long and anxious dwelling with experience and matter and the fluctuations of individual things, drags down the mind to earth or rather sinks it to a very Tartarus of turmoil and confusion; removing and withdrawing it from the serene tranquility of abstract wisdom, a condition far more heavenly. Now to this I readily assent; and indeed this which they point to as so much to be preferred, is the very thing of all other which I am about. For I am building in the human understanding a true model of the world, such as it is in fact, not such as man's own reason would have it to be; a thing which cannot be done without a very diligent dissection and anatomy of the world. But I say that those foolish and apish images of worlds which the fancies of men have created in philosophical systems, must be utterly scattered to the winds. Be it known how vast a difference there is

(as I said above) between the Idols of the human mind and the ideas of the divine. The former are nothing more than arbitrary abstraction; the latter are the creator's own stamp upon creation, impressed and defined in matter by true and exquisite lines. Truth, therefore, and utility are here the very same things; and works themselves are of a greater value as pledges of truth than as contributing to the comfort of life. (*Works*, I, 298)

At the beginning of his discussion of the relationship between truth and utility Bacon acknowledges that the study of the material world, as opposed to the "contemplation of truth," is associated with anxiety, confusion, and falling, and with Tartarus. Tartarus is the dark region located as far beneath Hades as Hades is from heaven, the region most absent from light—a common metaphor in Bacon's work for spiritual and intellectual knowledge. The opposition between earth as a kind of nothingness and the fullness of divine truth is a dichotomy which supports the doctrine of *contemptus mundi* that powerfully condemns human efforts to investigate the material world. Though Bacon's goal is to accomplish such an investigation, he follows a listing of the negative qualities traditionally attached to empirical study with, "Now to this I readily assent." At this moment Bacon links and separates himself from traditional doctrine. "This" is the voice of tradition; Bacon's submission to it seems to hazard his whole endeavor. His act of deference, however, elevates his project by allowing it to be enscribed within a metaphysical system. Once his project becomes traditional, tradition is transformed. While the symmetrical structure of the passage and Bacon's passive acquiescence lull us to sleep, Bacon performs a sleight of hand. The contemplation of truth is made equivalent to the study of the material world which had earlier seemed the antithesis of it.

The "Ideas of the divine," Bacon tells us, can only be discovered by anatomizing the world. This claim gives his anatomical method the privileged status of an absolutely reliable method of interpretation. With such an instrument at his disposal, Bacon gains the authority to expose former philosophical systems as "Idols" and replace them with the "true model" of science. He finishes by scattering old idols to the winds, thus dispersing the opposition to his new equation of truth and utility, theology and anatomy. Earlier anatomists inadvertently produced and discovered the decay of a traditional order—in the effort to cleanse the world by anatomizing it, they expanded the domain of worthless matter. Bacon intends to recuperate the old order by the very means that decomposed it in the first place. He is optimistic where his predecessors are pessimistic because he has found a way to reconcile empirical techniques and the "Ideas of the divine," or so he believes.

In spite of his shrewd analysis of the proclivity of men to establish insubstantial systems of order in place of truth, Bacon's own project was directed toward a utopia, a New Jerusalem.[5] It was important for the success of his ideas that this be so. The promise of absolute order helped subdue the fears of his audience about the consequence of a shift in the focus of knowledge from the contemplation of metaphysical truths to the contemplation of isolated facts which could not yet be placed within a formal system of knowledge. According to Bacon, "the fluctuations of individual things," the "turmoil and confusion" created by anatomizing matter, were not to be interpreted as signs of the decay of order, but as the precondition of its establishment. This new order was to be a genuine one, made of things themselves not empty words; it would be an order as ontologically secure as nature itself. Bacon locates it in a prelapsarian world where acts of language and knowledge are innocent, not yet separated from the truth of God and Nature. This placement of his project insures that the anatomist will not create "apish images" of the world. His representations will be real, true, chaste, "the creator's own stamp upon creation." As Bacon explains it in the *Advancement,* the scientist imitates Adam's acts of knowledge, "the view of creatures and the imposition of names," innocent acts of knowledge because, "As for the nature of the fall, it was . . . not the natural knowledge of creatures but the moral knowledge of good and evil" (*Works,* I, 61). Those who were unwilling to relinquish an archaic system of knowledge, a reluctance which was understandable given the incompleteness of Bacon's system, were seen by Bacon as obstacles to the achievement of an order more absolute than the traditional order of microcosm and macrocosm. His mission was to attack the men and their idols that stood in the way of the absolute "Instauration" of order.

It is not only the destruction of the old order but also the institution of the new one which receives a negative, repressive emphasis by Bacon. Bacon's description of his project is couched in a rhetoric of imperialism. "And surely it should be disgraceful if, while the regions of the material globe, — that is, of the earth, of the sea, and of the stars, — have been in our times laid widely open and revealed, the intellectual globe should remain shut up within the narrow limits of old discoveries" (*Works,* I, 282). As explorers and colonizers anatomize the world, laying it open to master it, so Bacon will lay open the intellectual world. The act of vision, described here as an anatomizing process, suggests the violence and disruption involved in such acts of discovery. The conquering power of the eye violates the integrity of the bodies of man, nature, and culture. So it is quite understandable that

Bacon himself compares the anatomizing process of discovery to war. The development of a military attitude toward the object of investigation is in fact one of the goals of Bacon's program to advance learning. No longer is learning to be an effeminate activity, a voluptuous playing with words. Instead, the man of knowledge will be an Alexander who uses his superior force to dominate space: "the arts that flourish while virtue is in growth are military; and while virtue is in declination are voluptuary" (*Works,* I, 108). By restoring truth Bacon will restore the "fierceness of men's minds" (*Works,* I, 71). As in earlier anatomies, masculine rhetoric and logic are opposed to deceitful feminine forms or painted "idols." In what seems like an act of sexual aggression, the anatomist penetrates those idols to reveal their falseness and insubstantiality. This act of penetrating the idols that ensnare men produces knowledge "for fruit or generation" (*Works,* I, 189).

Bacon recognizes that such acts of aggression can only be justified by his goal, the perfect restoration of knowledge. To fight against the tendency to make the destruction of idols an end in itself, he deliberately separates himself from anatomists like Democritus, to whom he admits he is indebted, because the school of Democritus is "so busied with the particulars that it hardly attends to the structure" (*Works,* I, 269). When all structures are dissected and nothing put in their place, then men begin to despair. And despair, Bacon says elsewhere, is the greatest obstacle to the progress of science (*Works,* I, 286). His recognition of the dark side of the anatomizing process, the way it breeds despair about reassembling a fragmented world, makes him turn from the demolition of idols to the task of enunciating the optimistic, utopian side of his project. As an antidote to despair, he offers hope not as a positive norm—Bacon is too much the anatomist to manage that—but as a promise that the limits of the mind and language—limits he so persuasively describes—will one day be overcome. Bacon offers several reasons for his hope that progress can be made in human understanding, the most important of which is the method of induction itself.

Bacon's strength, like that of earlier anatomists, lies less in the construction of a positive order, than in the destruction of false ones.[6] In the manner of all anatomies, his treatises are based on the assumption that appearances have become detached from reality and that the anatomist must therefore cut through these fictions to get to the truth. Bacon's skill at dissection is demonstrated in his exposure of the fallacies of man and language in the doctrine of the idols. He treats idols, in one form or another, in almost all of his works, because to reach the tangible, certain facts lying at the foundation of knowledge, he has first to tear away the superstitious notions that hide the truth from sight.

The negative process of destroying idols has a seductive power, as do many violent gestures of beginning, because it appears to make possible a complete break with the stale and limiting traditions of the past. Since idols "make the world the bond-slave of human thought, and human thought the bond-slave of words" (*Works,* I, 274), their destruction promises to give men a new power to know and speak the truth. Yet in spite of Bacon's hopeful efforts to be a liberator of men, his project seems faced with insurmountable obstacles. By his own admission, the idols of the tribe, cave, and marketplace are all innate and presumably resistant to his attack. And there is a more serious difficulty with his fragmenting way to reach the truth. What would happen if the idols actually were destroyed? The idols of the tribe have their origin in the mind's tendency to presuppose that its perceptions can be trusted and an origin in the will and affections; the idols of the cave are caused by the effects of nature and nurture; the idols of the marketplace are the result of the distortion caused by the inevitable gap between words and things; the idols of the theater are compelling orders of words that men substitute for nature itself. The eradication of these idols would constitute an apocalyptic sweeping away of all that makes up human culture. To abolish error and construct a new order, Bacon is embarked on a program to abolish "man," as we know him.

Bacon insists that his forceful clearing away of received ideas is a precondition for the advancement of learning. Yet on closer inspection Bacon's dissection of idols seems a ruthless—even murderous— activity, rather than a therapeutic one. In *The Masculine Birth of Time,* for example, the scientist as anatomist proclaims both his hostility to the enemies of progress and the virtue of ruthlessness:

> It is bad luck for me that, for lack of men, I must compare myself with brute beasts. But when you have had time to reflect you will see things differently. You will admire beneath the veil of abuse the spirit that has animated my attack. You will observe the skill with which I have packed every word with meaning and the accuracy with which I have launched my shafts straight into their hidden sores.[7]

There are two ways of interpreting Bacon's comparison of himself with beasts in this manifestation of his enthusiasm for dismembering his opponents. He may have intended to say that as a lone man among beasts he cannot be compared with other men. This maneuver to separate himself from beasts has the effect of placing him in the category he wants to avoid. Or he may mean that because no other man has dared to be as ferociously direct as he, he seems to be a beast. In any case, inadvertently or not, he acknowledges the brute violence of his own techniques. He also points to the virtuosity of his dissection as a mark of his superiority to the men he pierces with his shafts. From a man who elsewhere claims he would have his doctrine "enter quietly into minds that are fit and capable of receiving it" (*Works,* I, 263), the acts of negation on which his project depends seem unexpectedly harsh.

It is not only the destruction of the old order but also the institution of the new one which receives a negative, repressive emphasis by Bacon. Bacon's description of his project is couched in a rhetoric of imperialism. "And surely it should be disgraceful if, while the regions of the material globe,—that is, of the earth, of the sea, and of the stars,—have been in our times laid widely open and revealed, the intellectual globe should remain shut up within the narrow limits of old discoveries" (*Works,* I, 282). As explorers and colonizers anatomize the world, laying it open to master it, so Bacon will lay open the intellectual world. The act of vision, described here as an anatomizing process, suggests the violence and disruption involved in such acts of discovery. The conquering power of the eye violates the integrity of the bodies of man, nature, and culture. So it is quite understandable that Bacon himself compares the anatomizing process of discovery to war.

The development of a military attitude toward the object of investigation is in fact one of the goals of Bacon's program to advance learning. No longer is learning to be an effeminate activity, a voluptuous playing with words. Instead, the man of knowledge will be an Alexander who uses his superior force to dominate space: "the arts that flourish while virtue is in growth are military; and while virtue is in declination are voluptuary" (*Works,* I, 108). By restoring truth Bacon will restore the "fierceness of men's minds" (*Works,* I, 71). As in earlier anatomies, masculine rhetoric and logic are opposed to deceitful feminine forms or painted "idols." In what seems like an act of sexual aggression, the anatomist penetrates those idols to reveal their falseness and insubstantiality. This act of penetrating the idols that ensnare men produces knowledge "for fruit or generation" (*Works,* I, 189).

Bacon recognizes that such acts of aggression can only be justified by his goal, the perfect restoration of knowledge. To fight against the tendency to make the destruction of idols an end in itself, he deliberately separates himself from anatomists like Democritus, to whom he admits he is indebted, because the school of Democritus is "so busied with the particulars that it hardly attends to the structure" (*Works,* I, 269). When all structures are dissected and nothing put in their place, then men begin to despair. And despair, Bacon says elsewhere, is the greatest obstacle to the progress of science (*Works,* I, 286). His recognition of the dark side of the anatomizing process, the way it breeds despair about reassembling a fragmented world, makes him turn from the demolition of idols to the task of enunciating the optimistic, utopian side of his project. As an antidote to despair, he offers hope not as a positive norm—Bacon is too much the anatomist to manage that—but as a promise that the limits of the mind and language—limits he so persuasively describes—will one day be overcome. Bacon offers several reasons for his hope that progress can be made in human understanding, the most important of which is the method of induction itself.

In the traditional method of induction, a principle or opinion was shored up by supporting information rather than tested. Such a method cannot advance knowledge, and, according to Bacon, this proves its artificiality: "For what is founded on nature grows and increases; while what is founded on opinion varies but increases not" (*Works,* I, 274). For Bacon, nature becomes the external standard against which Bacon attempts to reinforce the "naturalness" of his method by establishing a correspondence between the stages of induction and what he says are the stages of human thinking: reception of sense data, classification of data, and finally interpretation of data.[8] But this correspondence between mind and method is misleading (an example of the mind's tendency to feign "correspondents and relations") not only because Bacon's definition of thinking is not substantiated but also because it disguises the fact that his method requires an assault on nature. The scientist who uses the method of induction must anatomize and distill objects in order to find the "forms" of nature: such qualities of matter as "dense, rare, hot, cold, heavy, light," that are supposed by Bacon to constitute an "alphabet" from which all natural compounds are made (*Works,* I, 469).[9] Forms are the basis of a perfect code of nature which, when made legible, will make nature totally comprehensible. The problem, as Bacon's practice shows, is that the endeavor to discover "forms" by anatomizing the world disrupts nature and generates a mass of contradictory information. In an attempt to control this information, Bacon provides a means of classification.

When Bacon searches for a form, he collects all the positive and negative instances of its occurrence and organizes them into "tables of discovery." As part of the process of discovering the form of heat, for example, he gives as a positive instance, "The rays of the sun, especially in summer and at noon." As a negative instance, he gives, "The rays of the moon and of stars and comets are not found to be hot to the touch" (*Works,* I, 308–09). Once all positive and negative instances are collected, the scientist simply eliminates contradictory instances until "there will remain at bottom, all light opinion vanishing into smoke, a Form affirmative, solid and true and well-defined" (*Works,* I, 320). The form of heat, then, should be a stable essence even if its outward attributes are relative and uncertain: "Heat as far as regards the sense and touch of man, is a thing various and relative; insomuch that tepid water feels hot if the hand be cold, but cold if the hand be hot" (*Works,* I, 320). Yet in spite of Bacon's promises, his process of discovery fails to conclude with the revelation of an affirmative form. The form of heat has neither form, nor visibility, nor tangibility. Bacon remarks: "For the heat and cold are not themselves perceptible to touch. . . . Nor . . . to the sight" (*Works,* I, 355). After removing "all ambiguity," he finds the form of heat is not a solid object but the ungraspable quality of "Motion."

Bacon believes motion is the form of heat because he has confidence in the efficacy of his tables of instances. In the characteristic manner of Bacon's writings, the tables are open structures which allow new information to be added and new conclusions to be made. Bacon's reliance on "tables of discovery" heralds a new age which replaced the traditional system of correspondences with a taxonomic system of order. According to Foucault, among the modifications in Western thought which resulted from this shift in modes of organizing is

the substitution of analysis for the hierarchy of analogies: in the sixteenth century, the fundamental supposition was that of a total system of correspondence (earth and sky, planets and faces, microcosm and macrocosm), and each particular similitude was then lodged within this overall relation. From now on, every resemblance must be subjected to proof by comparison, that is, it will not be accepted until its identity and the series of differences have been discovered by means of measurement with a common unit, or more radically by its position in an order. . . . A complete enumeration will now be possible: whether in the form of an exhaustive census of all the elements constituting the envisaged whole, or in the form of a categorical arrangement that will articulate the field of study in its totality.[10]

Bacon's treatises, unlike earlier, more rambling anatomies, attempt to provide a "categorical arrangement that will articulate the field of study in its totality," the field being nature itself. This is a herculean task, and Bacon's anatomizing technique for finding the basic elements of the natural order, a destructive rather than a constructive method of discovery, did not make it any easier to accomplish.

Bacon's emphasis on the negative instance, meant to insure impartial judgments, is an emphasis found in other anatomies, which, in proceeding by negatives, radically impede the imposition of order. Bacon is an heir to this tradition, even though his work is born of a desire to bring all nature under control. His works are governed by *antithesis,* a rhetorical device that maintains the "whirl and eddy of argument" that Bacon both abhors and abets. In an excellent article on the strategies Bacon employs in the *Essays* to disrupt a reader's preconceptions, Stanley Fish has shown that the operation of *antithesis* encourages the reader to suspend conclusions in order to scrutinize all the contradictory information available on a subject.[11] Rossi also comments on Bacon's preoccupation with *antitheta* as a means to check the mind's tendency to jump to conclusions.[12] In both cases *antithesis* apparently advances the cause of Bacon's new science. But the use of *antithesis* as a strategy for maintaining an argument (*Works,* I, 545–557) may lead not to progress in knowledge but to paralysis, an endless play of oppositions. The structure of Lyly's antithetical "Anatomy of Wit" demonstrates the danger of Bacon's plan to "proceed at first by negatives and at last to end in affirmatives" (*Works,* I, 320) — the process of negation endlessly postpones the arrival at synthesis. Many of Bacon's own works are a testament to the difficulty of reaching his goal, the final *Interpretation of Nature*: they are, by his own admission, fragments. Bacon's concern with the negative instance, with recording errors and cataloging monstrosities of nature, helped prove the incompleteness of existing explanations of nature. But that, of course, is not the same thing as providing a "true model of the world."

Bacon places a distance between his work and a rhetorical tour–de–force like Lyly's anatomy by attacking artificial systems of words and emphasizing the naturalness of his own project. He is attempting to create a science that "rests on the solid foundation of experience" which is unlike the literary sciences of the past which "float in the air" (*Works,* I, 154). In accord with his commitment to focus on empirical reality, he rejects witty forms of discourse that are full of words and far from nature itself. Bacon saw that the success of his method to discover the "true model of the world" depended on his ability to find a mode of communication that would enable him to overcome the limits of the idols of the marketplace which impede attempts to represent the world as it "really" is. The anatomy form encouraged the experiments in a style that Bacon conducted to create this new linguistic structure, as it had encouraged his critique of verbal structures. The anatomist sets out to dissect the idols of language because he suspects the integrity of words, and this very suspicion compels him to create new and hopefully more legitimate modes of communication—euphuism, the exploded verbal universe of Thomas Nashe, the aphoristic style of Sir Francis Bacon. All three men are preoccupied with language, but whereas the styles of Lyly and Nashe are self-consciously literary expressions of reality, Bacon's is a style that effaces itself in an effort to become capable of representing truths external to language.

An examination of Bacon's aphoristic style, a paradigmatic instance of the anatomical method, is useful for understanding the aims, effects, and shortcomings of the aphorism as a mode of scientific discourse. In the *Advancement* Bacon says that aphorisms "representing a knowledge broken do invite men to enquire further, whereas Methods carrying the shew of the total, do secure men as if they were at the furthest" (*Works,* I, 125). What Bacon means by "Methods" is not his own inductive method but traditional methods, such as the method of induction by enumeration or the syllogism, that encourage acceptance rather than critical examination of propositions. For example, of the syllogism he says:

> I . . . reject demonstration by syllogism, as acting too confusedly, and letting nature slip out of its hands. For although no one can doubt that things which agree in a middle term agree with one another (which is a proposition of mathematical certainty), yet it leaves an opening for deception; which is this. The syllogism consists of propositions; propositions of words; and words are tokens and signs of notions. Now if the notions of the mind (which are as the soul of words and the basis of the whole structure) be improperly and over-hastily abstracted from facts, vague, and not sufficiently definite, faulty in short in many ways, the whole edifice crumbles. (*Works,* I, 249)

Syllogistic logic is what Bacon calls a "magistral" method of communication that seduces the reader to accept as conclusions propositions that have never been proved. Magistral methods win consent because "they carry a kind of demonstration in orb or circle, one part illuminating another, and therefore satisfy" (*Works,* I, 125). In opposition to this method he proposes an "initiative" method which, like the inductive method, is a procedure to make all the data on which a conclusion is based available to the reader so that the reader can examine it for himself and test any conclusions drawn from it. It emphasizes particulars to help the reader "suspend Judgement" until the data have been reviewed. Aphorisms, says Bacon, present knowledge in "short and scattered sentences, not linked together by artificial method; and do not pretend or profess to embrace the entire art'' (*Works,* I, 283).

This statement about aphorisms reveals the same desire to go outside rhetoric to nature that motivates Bacon's invention of the method of induction to replace the rhetorical method of enumeration. But though he here claims that aphorisms make it possible for nature to be represented naturally, other remarks show that he was self-conscious about the ways a fragmentary style persuades a reader of the validity of material an author presents. Lisa Jardine, in *Francis Bacon: Discovery and Art of Discourse,* notes that Bacon himself discusses the way ''unordered division of material gives the effect of profusion; ordered division adds the illusion that the coverage is complete, and the limits of investigation set.''[13] She adds that Bacon favors aphorism because ''unordered division also conveys the impression that there is further material to be investigated.'' Profusion and lack, these are the effects of aphoristic style, independent of content. In *De Augmentis* Bacon argues against the fallacy that ''that which consists of many divisible parts is greater than that which consists of a few parts and is more one'' (*Works,* I, 617). His critical dissection of the style of fragments is even more pronounced in *The Masculine Birth of Time* in which he attacks the wisdom of Hippocrates conveyed in aphorisms. Hippocrates, he says, protects himself from scrutiny ''according to the fashion of his age by an oracular brevity. . . . But in truth the oracle is dumb. He utters nothing but a few sophisms sheltered from correction by their curt ambiguity.''[14] These shrewd objections to the aphoristic method make readers more confident in Bacon's ability to avoid the snares of aphorisms when he uses them himself. After all, his aphorisms, unlike those of Hippocrates, are apparently uncompromised by an artificial linguistic arrangement.

But it is Bacon's recognition that language is always an artificial order that compels his persistent efforts to avoid it. In fact, a mistrust of even mathematical languages encouraged him to develop a system of investigation, the inductive method, that appears to begin from scratch. His use of aphorisms was also designed to reduce language to a minimum in order to bring the content of a proposition to a maximum. In other words, he reduces both nature and language so language will seem unobtrusive and nature undeniably present. But as Bacon's own objections to what he calls ''ridiculous'' aphorisms show, there is no reason to assume that the content and value of a proposition will increase if the number of words it contains is as small as possible (*Works,* I, 125). The very compactness of aphorisms may instead make them enigmatic or ''oracular'' rather than clear and straightforward.

Bacon admits he values a veiled method of communication in his studies of fables and parables but he does not comment on the hiero-glyphic character of his own aphorisms. He does say that nature is a labyrinth, and, since he says often that his method mirrors nature, we may take this as a warning. Aphorisms are like hieroglyphs because they are dark, "oracular," forms which, like nature itself, must be anatomized if their hidden meaning is to be revealed. They are also a similitude, a visual hieroglyph, of the particulars of nature. Hiero-glyphs, as Bacon notes, both hide meaning and reveal it (*Works, I,* 441). An aphorism demands dissection as a way to reveal its hidden truth; but it also illustrates the solid kernel of fact which remains after a dissection has been made. Its contradictory message is another hiero-glyph, a sign of Bacon's transitional position between traditional and modern styles of knowledge. The aphorism is the zero point where science and alchemy come together—it not only makes nature present, it also defers that presencing by veiling nature. This veiled form entices the reader to participate with Bacon in an alchemical delving into the mysteries of nature. The "pith and heart of the sciences" is also the philosopher's stone of the alchemist.

As we have seen, these two sides of Bacon's science are evident not only in the aphorism but also in the negative instance which allows and postpones the discovery of an affirmative form, and in the use of *antithesis* to prevent the mind from jumping to false conclusions, or arriving at true ones. This doubleness, though it impedes construction of the "true model" of science, gives his project rhetorical force. The man who uses Bacon's methods has the power to dispel illusion and to create the illusion, the dream, of a future in which mute objects will speak truths that will make all things possible. These two poles of his project, scientific and alchemical, justify science and inspire faith in its telos.

Faith that an "anatomy of the world" will lead to "utility and fruit" links Bacon's method to power as well as truth. Earlier anatomists had complained that knowledge was severed from power. Lyly and Nashe, for example, suffered from a sense that learning was not valued by society and this prompted them to attack their own education as well as the people in power who neglected learned men like themselves. The estrangement of the anatomist is marked by their anatomies: Euphues goes into exile; Nashe's anatomist is an alienated, discontented scholar. But Bacon, though critical of traditional learning, places the man who anatomizes tradition at the heart of society, a place perhaps equivalent to his own, lord chancellor of England. He is at the center because a technique of criticism, anatomizing, has been endowed with the capa-city to control the wealth of nature. The new anatomist is a figure of magnificence as Bacon's description of the scientist in the *New Atlantis* shows:

> He was a man of middle stature and age, comely of person, and had an aspect as if he pitied men. He was clothed in a robe of fine black cloth, with wide sleeves and a cape. His garment was of excellent white linen down to the foot, girt with a girdle of the same; and a sindon or tippet of the same about his neck. He had gloves that were curious, and set with stone; and shoes of peach-colored velvet. . . . He was carried in a rich chariot without wheels litter-wise; with two horses at either end, richly trapped in blue velvet embroidered, and two footmen on each side in the like attire. The chariot was all of cedar, gilt, and adorned with crystal; save the fore-end had pannels of sapphires, set in borders of gold, and the hinder-end the like of emeralds of the Peru color. (*Works*, III, 154–55)

His knowledge, symbolized by a "sun of gold radiant upon the top," dazzles as much as his possessions do. One depends on the other. The scientist is given wealth because his knowledge is valuable, his knowledge leads to the production of the wealth he is given in payment. No one begrudges him absolute rule.

The visage of the "Father of Saloman" suggests, though, that his eminence exacts a cost: he has an "aspect as if he pitied men." The importance of method is only comprehensible if one grasps the limits of human intelligence and the necessity of "helps." As Bacon says, "if I have made any progress, the way has been opened to me by no other than the true and legitimate humiliation of the human spirit" (*Works*, I, 246). In order to find the lucrative truth of nature, one must paradoxically accept the estrangement of human perception and language from nature. Where earlier anatomists had separated themselves from society, now the separation is internalized; the intellect is separated from nature rather than the individual from society. This estrangement marks the shift from the order of microcosm and macrocosm to the order of taxonomy. The mistrust of apparent resemblances between the world of man and of nature, words and things, led to the proliferation of anatomies which cut through appearances, breaking objects down into the simplest elements which were then rearranged in a taxonomic order quite different from the apparent order of the world that had once been so full of significance. The cost of this shift, as Timothy Reiss puts it, was not only a loss of "confidence in Man's energies, in his capacity to seize and conduct the world around him in his own name," but the revelation of the insufficiencies of our sense impressions and of the impossibility of our basing any intellectual systems of the external world upon them. A contract between mind and matter was lost. Man placed himself to one side of matter."[15] That break between mind and matter, language and nature, could not be bridges within language itself, even the carefully formed language structures of Bacon's new science.

The ending of the old and the beginning of a new relation between man and language is the subject of Hugo von Hoffmansthal's "The Letter of Lord Chandos." The letter, supposedly from Lord Chandos, an English gentleman, to Bacon, is written to explain why Lord Chandos will never write again. The implications of the doctrine of the idols have overwhelmed him. Lord Chandos had once been a passionate man of letters, a man much like Bacon himself, who wrote plays, pastorals, and Latin treatises, and entertained plans to write a history of Henry VIII, to decipher the fables of the ancients, to write an encyclopedic book unlocking the mysteries of nature:

> To sum up: In those days I, in a state of continuous intoxication, conceived the whole existence as one great unit: the spiritual and the physical worlds seemed to form no contrast, as little as did courtly and bestial conduct, art and barbarism, solitude and society; in everything I felt the presence of Nature, in the aberrations of insanity as much as in the utmost refinement of the Spanish ceremonial; in the boorishness of young peasants no less than in the most delicate of allegories; and in all expressions of Nature I felt myself. When in my hunting lodge I drank the warm foaming milk which an unkempt wench had drained into a wooden pail from the udder of a beautiful gentle-eyed cow, the sensation was no different from that which I experienced when, seated on a bench built into the window of my study, my mind absorbed the sweet foaming nourishment from a book. The one was like the other, whether in dreamlike celestial quality or in physical intensity—and thus it prevailed through the whole expanse of life in all directions; everywhere I was in the centre of it, never suspecting mere appearance.[16]

His use of the past tense indicates that appearances have become suspect. A sense that words are separate from the presence of Nature compels him to look more closely at language and the men that use it: he conducts an anatomy. But here anatomy is not a construct with positivity: "For me everything disintegrated into parts, and those parts again to parts, no longer would anything let itself be encompassed by one idea.''[17] Occasionally Lord Chandos could find consolation in natural images of isolation and entrapment—a cripple, rats locked in a poisoned cellar—that linked him again to the external world. Finally he decided that to reappropriate presence he must eschew all forms of mediation: Lord Chandos embraces silence.

One can imagine Bacon, after reading this letter, composing a note to his friend prescribing the ministrations of his method as the means to overcome the inadequacy of words. He could remain calm in the face of anxiety generated from his own doctrines because his dream of order protected him from the knowledge that anatomizing nature might destroy it, or the possibility that anatomizing opened up a problematic relation between words and things that compromises his own work as well as that of the ancients. Bacon was more right than he knew when he speculated that some day future generations would say of him what a Roman historian had said of Alexander: "All Alexander did was dare to despise shams."[18] Bacon despised the false orders that serve for our reality but could not replace them with "real" ones. What he bequeathed to the centuries that followed was an insatiable desire to enclose nature and an anatomizing method which was both the means and the obstacle to satisfying that desire. Modern science, and the disciplines it has sponsored, are heirs to the satisfactions and frustrations of Bacon's desire and his methods.

The University of Wyoming

NOTES

1. Reference to Bacon's writings, with the exception of *The Masculine Birth of Time* and *The Refutation of Philosophies*, are from the *The Works of Francis Bacon*, vol. I, ed. James Spedding and Robert Ellis (London: George Routledge and Sons, 1905) and vols. III and V, ed. James Spedding, Robert Ellis, and Douglas D. Heath (London: Longman and Co., 1889). Throughout my text these writings will be referred to as *Works* with volume and page number.

2. Loren C. Eisely, *The Man Who Saw Through Time* (New York: Scribner, 1973), p. 70.

3. Thomas Nashe, "The Anatomie of Absurditie," *The Works of Thomas Nashe*, ed. Ronald B. McKerrow, vol. I (Oxford: Basil Blackwell, 1958), p. 9.

4. Marshall McLuhan, in "Francis Bacon: Ancient or Modern?" (*Renaissance and Reformation* 10 [1974]), argues that Bacon approached science "in the spirit of the ancient grammarians and observers of the page of nature" (p. 94).

5. As Puritan beliefs in man's wickedness encouraged movements of reformation, so

Bacon's view of man's limitations compelled him to devise a method for overcoming those limitations and establishing a new order on earth.

6. C. S. Lewis says of Bacon that he is best "not as discoverer of truths but as exposer of fallacies." See his *English Literature in the Sixteenth Century Excluding Drama* (Oxford: Clarendon Press, 1954), p. 537.

7. Sir Francis Bacon, "The Masculine Birth of Time," trans. Benjamin Farrington, *The Philosophy of Francis Bacon* (Liverpool: Liverpool University Press, 1974), p. 70.

8. Lisa Jardine makes a similar observation in *Francis Bacon: Discovery and the Art of Discourse* (London: Cambridge University Press, 1974), p. 96.

9. Brian Vickers remarks that "Bacon's increasing use of natural, organic images for knowledge modifies the implications of an 'anatomy', for instead of cutting-up nature we are presented with the idea of division as being a temporary highlighting of a branch within the fundamental unity of the sciences." See his *Francis Bacon and Renaissance Prose* (Cambridge: Cambridge University Press, 1968), p. 56.

10. Michel Foucault, *The Order of Things: An Archaeology of the Human Sciences* (New York: Vintage, 1970), pp. 54–55.

11. See Stanley E. Fish, *Self-Consuming Artifacts* (Berkeley and Los Angeles: University of California Press, 1972), pp. 78–144.

12. Paolo Rossi, *Francis Bacon: From Magic to Science*, trans. Sacha Rabinovitch (Chicago: University of Chicago Press, 1968), p. 182.

13. P. 176.

14. Bacon, "The Masculine Birth of Time," p. 68.

15. Timothy J. Reiss, "Introduction: The Word/World Equation," *Yale French Studies* 49 (1973), p. 6.

16. Hugo von Hofmannsthal, "The Letter of Lord Chandos," in *Selected Prose,* trans. Mary Hottinger, Tania Stern, and James Stern (New York: Pantheon Books, 1952), p. 32.

17. Ibid., p. 134.

18. Sir Francis Bacon, "The Refutation of Philosophies," in *The Philosophy of Francis Bacon* (see note 7), p. 132.

The Amorous Girl–Boy: Sexual Ambiguity in Thomas Lodge's *Rosalynde*

Janice Paran

*R*osalynde, Thomas Lodge's pastoral novel, appeared in 1590. The occasion would hardly be of interest to us today, the book being merely a popular romance of the period, were it not for the fact that it provided Shakespeare with a story for *As You Like It*. Rosalynde, daughter of the exiled king of France, is banished by her usurping uncle. Disguised as a boy and accompanied by her cousin Alinda, she finds sanctuary in the Forest of Arden, where she encounters her beloved Rosader, who, of course, does not recognize her. Rosader has likewise sought shelter in the forest, because his brother, jealous over an inheritance, has tried to kill him. Various complications, cross-purposes, and costume confusions ensue, until at length the rightful king is restored to his throne, Rosader is reconciled to his brother, and Rosalynde and Rosader marry.

This, essentially, is also the scenario for the action of *As You Like It*, though Shakespeare changed some names and added a few characters. Thus *Rosalynde* has earned perennial passing mention in literary criticism and in countless introductions to editions of *As You Like It:* as Shakespeare's source. The plot of *Rosalynde*, however, is not Lodge's only legacy. Sexual ambiguity, a subject used consciously and brilliantly by Shakespeare in his treatment of the tale, is also *Rosalynde's* most intriguing, if inadvertent, characteristic.

The idea that appearances deceive, while not exactly startling in originality, is a fundamental theme of the novel. That much is clear from its aphorisms alone. There are dozens of them. Nearly every character makes a habit of reciting them; Lodge's own narrative is rife with them. "Low shrubs have deep roots, and poor cottages great patience." "When the licorice leaf looketh dry, then it is most wet:

91

when the shores of Lepanthus are most quiet, then they forepoint a storm." "Of all flowers the rose is the fairest, and yet guarded with the sharpest prickles."[1] These doses of philosophy are applied to every sort of emotion, event, decision, and circumstance. They are nearly all cautionary adages, reminders that appearances are untrustworthy, that oppositions are everywhere found. Such caveats are verbal armor in a world understood to be fundamentally hostile to human endeavor, where intelligent forces plot to thwart human effort. "Be careful," warn these epigrams, "at every step, there's a snare." At the same time, the world of *Rosalynde* provides no reliable ethos, no scheme of responsibility. Its characters invoke Nature, Fortune, and Fate frequently and almost interchangeably, as if to summon the widest range of insurance against calamity. Underlying Lodge's skipping pastoral, it could be argued, is a decidedly grim understanding of human existence and its place in the universe.

It is not my purpose here, however, to explore Lodge's cosmography. In the first place, I am not sure he is worth the effort. A certain metaphysical paradox may be gleaned from *Rosalynde*—oaths are as vehement as they are ineffectual—but only incidentally. Lodge himself seems unaware of the disquieting undercurrent; unlike Shakespeare, he does not incorporate it into his subject. But his muddled world view, albeit unconscious, is extremely interesting in its effect. The hazards of fate, essential to the tragic vision, take a comic form in *Rosalynde:* the vagaries of love are perplexing but harmless. Lodge's narrative, in its creation of a blithely chaotic universe, fixes no culpability for the amorous adventures (or rather, names several guilty parties—Cupid, Venus, Folly, Fortune—which comes to the same thing). What is important is the confounding of characters and intents, and Lodge's Forest of Arden puts its oppositional adages to the test. Things are not always or only what they seem, in Lodge's forest as surely as in Shakespeare's, especially in the realm of sexuality.

Sexual ambiguity is centered, of course, in the person of Rosalynde. Her sexual identity assumes no fewer than five variations in the course of the novel. In the beginning, while she is still at court and before she has fallen under Rosader's spell, her sexuality is adolescent. Her closest companion and confidante is her cousin Alinda. They are "bed-fellows in royalty" (p. 33); they share the devoted homosexual bond of adolescence. Upon their exile, Rosalynde disguises herself as a man, calls herself Ganymede, and she and Alinda (now Aliena) set up rural housekeeping. They establish, in effect, a homosexual marriage, with Rosalynde as the husband. As Ganymede, Rosalynde befriends Rosader, and theirs is a men's companionship. But when Ganymede impersonates Rosalynde for Rosader to woo, another homosexual bond (this time male) is suggested. Finally, when Rosalynde's true identity is revealed and she weds Rosader, she embodies mature heterosexuality; for the first time, she is a "genuine" woman. In stages, then, she passes from girl to pretend man, "real" man, "pretend" woman, and finally to real woman. In only the first and last of these phases is her sexuality single-faceted. Significantly, these are the periods when she is not living in the forest. The forest is the liminal region; there her sexuality is ambiguous, hermaphroditic. The phenomenon is far more complex than the device of a woman in a man's clothing. It is not deception, but a partial transformation.

Shakespeare was able to assume an additional level of sexual ambiguity in the creation of his Rosalind by virtue of the fact that the part would be played by a boy. Lodge wrote a novel; he had no such corporeal paradox. What he does have is language. The most important component of the ambiguity created by Lodge is grammatical. Lodge does not, as might be expected, continue to refer to Rosalynde as Rosalynde even when she is disguised. (The *reader* of *As You Like It,* incidentally, is slightly handicapped in appreciating the blurring of genders, since Rosalind's speeches are always labeled "Rosalind.") With a few exceptions (to be dealt with shortly), once Rosalynde dons a page's apparel, Lodge's narrative refers to her as Ganymede and, more importantly, uses masculine pronouns. While this linguistic convention is common in romance literature, its effect upon the reader's imagination must be noted. "She" would remind the reader that Rosalynde is a woman; "he" informs the reader that Ganymede is a man. Not impersonation, but transmutation. A pronoun accomplishes the impossible, effecting a paradox more completely than even Shakespeare's stage could hope to. The initial shift is simple and astonishing:

> At this Alinda smiled, and upon this they agreed, and presently gathered up all their jewels, which they trussed up in a casket, and Rosalynde in all haste provided her of robes, and Alinda, from her royal weeds, put herself in more homelike attire. Thus fitted to the purpose, away go these two friends, having now changed their names, Alinda being called Aliena, and Rosalynde Ganymede. They travelled along the vineyards. . . . Passing thus on along, about midday they came to a fountain. . . . By this fountain sat Aliena and her Ganymede, and forth they pulled such victuals as they had, and fed as merrily as if they had been in Paris with all the

king's delicates, Aliena only grieving that they could not so much as meet with a shepherd to discourse them the way to some place where they might make their abode. At last Ganymede casting up his eye espied where on a tree was engraven certain verses; which as soon as he espied, he cried out. (Pp. 34–35)

Disguised as Ganymede, Rosalynde takes on traditionally masculine attributes: pragmatism, jocularity, and unsentimentality. It is Ganymede who tends the flocks, converses confidently with Rosader, and deals harshly with Phoebe, the shepherdess who has rejected the suit of an adoring swain and turned her attentions to Ganymede ("And if, damsel, you fled from me, I should transform you as Daphne to a bay, and then in contempt trample your branches under my feet" [p. 121]). At other times, it is Rosalynde's conventionally feminine personality which prevails, as she pines for Rosader, hiding her passion "in the cinders of honourable modesty" (p. 67). More fascinating than the instances of a predominating sexuality, though, are the occasions of ambiguity, when Rosalynde and Ganymede are indistinguishable or at least instantaneously interchangeable, when they form what Lodge once calls "the amorous girl-boy" (p. 123). Rosalynde/Ganymede becomes a true androgyne, a beautiful youth, half boy and half girl, or more accurately, a mysterious mutation that is at the same time a boyish girl and a girlish boy. Lodge creates his lovely monster most strikingly and probably inadvertently when he slips from one name and/or gender into the other within the same passage. It is worth quoting several instances of this peculiar verbal magic:

Ganymede, who still had the remembrance of Rosader in his thoughts, took delight to see the poor shepherd passionate, laughing at Love, that in all his actions was so imperious. At last, when she had noted his tears that stole down his cheeks . . . she demanded of Corydon why the young shepherd looked so sorrowful. (P. 48)

Ganymede had tears in her eyes, and passions in her heart to see her Rosader so pained, and therefore stepped hastily to the bottle, and filling out some wine in a mazer, she . . . gave it him, which did comfort Rosader, that rising, with the help of his brother, he took his leave of them, and went to his lodge. Ganymede, as soon as they were out of sight, led his flocks down to a vale, and there under the shadow of a beech tree sate down, and began to mourn the misfortunes of her sweetheart. (P. 108)

Straight, as women's heads are full of wiles, Ganymede had a
fetch to force Phoebe to fancy the shepherd, malgrado the resolution of her mind: he prosecuted his policy thus. (P. 142)

Thus, all three content, and soothed up in hope, Ganymede took
his leave of his Phoebe and departed, leaving her a contented
woman, and Montanus highly pleased. But poor Ganymede, who
had her thoughts on her Rosader . . . filled her eyes full of tears,
and her heart full of sorrows. (P. 146)

The richness of the ambiguity is epitomized in the courtship and mock
marriage between Rosader and Ganymede, a sequence Shakespeare
highlights in *As You Like It*. Ganymede, to tease and cheer the lovelorn
Rosader, "plays" Rosalynde for him. Ganymede's Rosalynde is a
good-natured parody of female behavior: she hesitates, demands proof
of her lover's honorable intentions, but finally favors his suit. Ganymede enjoys the jest:

How now, forester, have I not fitted your turn? have I not played
the woman handsomely, and myself as coy in grants as courteous
in desires, and been as full of suspicion as men of flattery? and yet
to salve all, jumped I not all up with the sweet union of love? Did
not Rosalynde content her Rosader? (Pp. 89-90)

The irony, of course, is that Ganymede *is* Rosalynde, and so her coy-
ness is both feigned and genuine. Further, since Rosalynde hides her
identity from Rosader, she is guilty of deception in a very specific sense,
though Ganymede swears that Rosalynde, if she knew Rosader, could
not be unfair. Sexual distinctions have all but evaporated in this scene.
This androgynous creature, this woman playing a man playing a
woman, exhibits "male" and "female" traits at the same time: (s)he is
straightforward, coquettish, virtuous, fickle, sporting, and smug.

The mock nuptials take the sexual confusion one more fantastic step.
Ganymede, who has been a kind of husband to Aliena, is now made
Rosader's wife. (Aliena performs the ceremony, in effect pimping for
her "mate.") The marriage is stranger still, for as Aliena informs
Rosader, "I must carry this night the bride with me" (pp. 91-92). On
Ganymede's wedding night, Rosader's bride is Aliena's groom.
Rosalynde/Ganymede is both halves of the wedding; she partners her-
self. The semantic accident of the word "bridegroom" happens to
describe her exactly.

Rosalynde/Ganymede's ambisexual appeal is manifestly clear in the novel's comic love triangle as well as in Shakespeare's borrowing of it. Rosalynde is the object of Rosader's affections, Ganymede of Phoebe's. The face and body (clothed, of course) are the same; only the sexual filter, the perception of the viewer or reader, changes. Androgyny as an ideal of the sexual imagination, of which the romance tradition is only one province of representation, is the model implicit in *Rosalynde* and later in *As You Like It*. A line of Ganymede's states the enchanting proposition:

> Who knows not, but that all women have desire to tie sovereignty to their petticoats, and ascribe beauty to themselves, where, if boys might put on their garments, perhaps they would prove as comely. (P. 72)

Descriptions of beauty's perfection in a woman are almost identical to the descriptions of a man's beauty. Rosalynde/Ganymede embodies the ideal in boyish womanhood or girlish manhood. Compare this description of Rosalynde:

> Upon her cheeks there seemed a battle between the Graces, who should bestow most favours to make her excellent. The blush that glories Luna, when she kissed the shepherd on the hills of Latmos, was not tainted with such a pleasant dye as the vermilion flourished on the silver hue of Rosalynde's countenance: her eyes were like those lamps that make the wealthy covert of the heavens more gorgeous, sparkling favour and disdain, courteous and yet coy, as if in them Venus had placed all her amorets, and Diana all her chastity. The trammels of her hair, folded in a caul of gold, so far surpassed the burnished glister of the metal, as the sun doth the meanest star in brightness . . . she was the paragon of all earthly perfection. (Pp. 16-17)

to this of Ganymede:

> She called to mind the several beauties of young Ganymede; first his locks, which being amber-hued, passeth the wreath that Phoebus puts on to make his front glorious; his brow of ivory was like the seat where love and majesty sits enthroned to enchain fancy; his eyes as bright as the burnishing of the heaven, darting forth frowns with disdain and smiles with favour, lightning such looks as would inflame desire, were she wrapped in the circle of the frozen zone; in his cheeks the vermilion teinture of the rose

flourished upon natural alabaster, the blush of the morn and Luna's silver show were so lively portrayed, that the Troyan that fills out wine to Jupiter was not half so beautiful. . . . The idea of these perfections tumbling in her mind made the poor shepherdess . . . perplexed. (Pp. 133–34)

It is the same beauty that inflames Rosader for Rosalynde and Phoebe for Ganymede. The boy/girl appeal is a transparently erotic one, but it is ironic that Rosalynde and Ganymede must remain chaste for as long as they are joined in a single body. The sexuality of the androgyne is both immediate and remote: Rosalynde/Ganymede is the specific object of intense sexual desire; (s)he is also unattainable. The sexuality of the forest is in a state of suspended frustration; no consummation is possible. Actual sexual contact is the end of ambiguity: a body is either male or female. Chastity is the promise of possibility. The revelation of Rosalynde's true identity must destroy Ganymede. Sexuality is clarified as the characters prepare to move out of the forest—out of the liminal into the world of definition and hierarchy.

Drew University

NOTES

1. *Lodge's 'Rosalynde' Being the Original of Shakespeare's 'As You Like It'*, ed. W. W. Greg (London: Oxford University Press, 1931), pp. 4, 51. All subsequent citations are to this edition and appear parenthetically.

Audiences and Rhetorical Strategies in Jodelle, Shakespeare, and Lohenstein

William J. Kennedy

odelle wrote his *Cleopatre Captive* (1553) when he was twenty years old and fresh from the tutelage of Muret and Dorat. Shakespeare wrote his *Antony and Cleopatra* (1607) when he was forty-three and at the height of his theatrical career. Lohenstein wrote his *Cleopatra* (1661, revised in 1680) when he was forty-five and for many years an active syndic and advocate in the Council of Breslau. The first play was designed for a coterie performance before an audience of the king and royal followers. The second was designed for commercial performances during the summer before a popular audience outdoors at London's Globe Theater, and later during the winter before a genteel audience indoors at the Blackfriars Theater. The third was written for school performances before a select bourgeois audience of patrons and professionals in a city that had yet no resident theater. A complex pattern of interaction among tradition, text, and audience in these plays has significance for literary history, and it makes a comparison of their unequal dramatic results worthwhile.

The concepts of tradition, text, and audience all display firm roots in classical rhetoric.[1] Each of them has in turn acquired a modern meaning in its own right. Within a hermeneutic framework articulated by Heidegger and Gadamer, for example, tradition is more than the handing down of a dead mass; it entails the placing of oneself within a process of understanding in which the past and present are constantly fused.[2] Nor does the structure of the text represent any simple appropriation of ideal types. For Russian Formalism and its semiotic heirs, it incorporates modal and stylistic properties that modify generic ones in a dynamic manner, so that it subsists on several levels at once. Thus, according to Roman Ingarden's formulation, the text presents itself in various aspects that each member of the audience "concretizes" in a specific way.[3] With the audience, a variety of contemporary approaches attempts to determine its role in apprehending the text. They range from sociological reception studies (Jauss, Weimann) to formal and stylistic analyses (Iser, Fish), and from detailed linguistic studies (Jakobson) to wholly subjective approaches (Bleich). In historical investigations, however, it is most helpful to distinguish between auditors or readers in specific performances or concretizations and the "fictive audience" that the author has incorporated into the text. Walter Ong's epithet, "the writer's audience is always a fiction," epitomizes this distinction.[4]

In Jodelle's, Shakespeare's, and Lohenstein's plays about Cleopatra, these factors raise complicated issues. Their tradition reaches back to a single text, Plutarch's *Life of Marc Antony*. With its own indeterminacies and ambiguities, that text lends itself readily to various treatments evident even in its mediating translations by Leonardo Aretino (into Latin, 1496), Claude de Seyssel (into French, 1544), and Thomas North (into English, 1579).[5] Jodelle, Shakespeare, and Lohenstein used these translations, and they may also have referred to still other ancient accounts by Dio Cassius and Appian. More importantly they evoked literary analogues of Cleopatra. In Roman literature there were Horace's ironic Ode on Cleopatra (I.37), Vergil's tragic Dido (with Vergil's forecast of the battle of Actium in *Aeneid* (VIII.675-728), and Ovid's pathetic heroines in the *Heroides*. In later literature there are countless references, as a topos, to Cleopatra's improper subordination of honor to lust or femininity, as in the pictures on the gate of Armida's garden in Tasso's *Gerusalemme liberata* (XVI.4-7). There were also, of course, many dramatizations of the story. Jodelle may have had access to the Italian plays by Alessandro Spinelli (*Cleopatra*, 1540), Giraldi Cinthio (*Cleopatra*, 1543), and Cesare de' Cesari (*Cleopatra tragedia*, 1552); and Shakespeare, to Robert Garnier's *Marc Antoine* (1578, translated into English by the Countess of Pembroke, 1590), and Samuel Daniel's *Cleopatra* (1594). Concretizing these texts and others, the playwrights as readers allow them to grow together with the tradition, as the Latin etymology of the verb, *con-crescere*, implies.[6] For creative authors composing new texts, the possibilities of extending the tradition increase in geometrical proportion to the availability of older texts.

These possibilities entail formal choices. The textual forms embracing the tradition of the Cleopatra plays range from biographies and histories to epics and lyrics, and they include translations and adaptations as well as original plays. Each form has its own generic, modal, and stylistic properties, but often they fuse in unexpected ways. The history of any given genre shows how its adjacent modes and styles develop in different directions at different rates of speed, and the three Cleopatra plays at hand exemplify that historical principle. Within the temporal span of slightly more than a century, they incorporate various formal techniques of European drama. The structural roots of Jodelle's play lie in French courtly literature and early academic classicism of the mid-sixteenth century, Shakespeare's in the popular conventions of late Elizabethan theater, and Lohenstein's in German academic, courtly, and bourgeois culture in the second half of the seventeenth century. Their ideological superstructures, however, go beyond merely formal techniques. Jodelle's play is more than a tragedy of fallen fortunes on the classical model, Shakespeare's is more than a casual entertainment, and Lohenstein's is more than a dazzling Baroque display of reversal and counterreversal.

The relationships of their audiences with the texts and traditions then becomes highly problematic. Just as each text projects a role or series of roles to be played by the characters in articulating the playwright's point of view, so it also projects roles to be played by the audience. Its roles are as fictive as the ones assigned to the play's characters. They demand of the audience an active commitment to enter the world of the play in a careful, studied manner.[7] They may reflect the temporal conditions of the text's origin, when the creative moment dictated its production for a particular kind of historical audience. They may also reflect the temporal conditions of its present reception so that we understand it to address us now, in quite a different way. In both cases these fictive roles require the members of the audience to share certain attitudes towards the text and its tradition. They are not necessarily those of the nobles in Jodelle's King's Chamber in 1553, nor the groundlings in Shakespeare's pit in 1607, nor Lohenstein's Silesian schoolboys and their bourgeois families in 1661, but they do need careful examination and articulation in approaching the plays' literary history.

The diverse members of Jodelle's coterie audience, for example, must share attitudes towards the text and tradition that are at once academic, cultivated, courtly, and aristocratic. This audience differs significantly from that of the playwright's traditional source, Plutarch. The latter addressed philosophically educated readers prepared to accept Platonic advice on ethics and politics. The *Lives* were a text for thoughtful meditation and disinterested contemplation. Jodelle addresses an audience with a more pragmatic and wordly orientation. He makes the play function as a courtroom drama where the audience must weigh the characters' rhetoric more than their actions. The audience must judge the characters as though they were on trial less for what they have done than for what they say they are doing.

The aims that guide Jodelle here and elsewhere certainly are not slouching toward the psychological conventions of seventeenth-century classical drama to be born. Neither author nor audience is at all interested in the norms of complex motivation, the three unities, *bienséances,* or most other aspects of good taste that would characterize plays by Mairet, Rotrou, and Corneille. Instead Jodelle plots his play's action primarily to fulfill the norm of rhetorical exploration.[8] In the prologue dedicating the play to Henri II, he calls attention to its language and its rhetoric with the claim that no French author has yet duplicated the language of ancient tragedy:

> Nous t'apportons (o bien petit hommage)
> Ce bien peu d'oeuvre ouvre de ton langage,
> Mais tel pourtant que ce langage tien,
> N'avoit jamais derobbe ce grand bien
> Des auteurs vieus.
>
> (Prologue, 33–37) [9]

[We bring you a homage small enough—this little bit of work wrought from your own language, but yet in such a way that your language had never reaped the profit of ancient authors.]

Its inquiring mode emphasizes the king's presence as chief rhetorical arbiter. It does so at least textually in the prologue, and it probably did so theatrically in the play's first performance, when the king in attendance sat prominently near the stage. In viewing the play the audience would have viewed the king viewing—and judging—the play. Its own rule, modeled on the royal one, would have been to follow the action with the same perspicacity that one would expect of such an arbiter. The aim is to make each member of the audience respond to the rhetoric as a sovereign magistrate.

The bravado of the characters' language everywhere stimulates this kind of response. It has the capacity to reveal and conceal private motivations, to lead and mislead public opinion, and to form and deform human experience. Through it Antoine justifies the gods' vengeance on him for having preferred Cleopatre to his wife and children, but he also manages to find an excuse for his conduct:

> Car un ardent amour, bourreau de mes mouelles,
> Me devorant sans fin sous ses flames cruelles,
> Avoit este commis par quelque destinee
> Des Dieux jalous de moy, a fin que terminee
> Fust en peine et malheur ma pitoyable vie.
>
> (I.69–73)

[A burning love, the torment of my very marrow, consuming me endlessly in its cruel flames, has been sent by fate from the gods who are jealous of me, to end my pitiable life in pain and misfortune.]

By externalizing the "ardent amour" as a vengeance sent by the gods, he accepts his punishment and at the same time mitigates his guilt. Cleopatre likewise justifies her embrace of death. The text indicates her captivity to the same rhetorical habits as Antonine's:

> Vne eternelle nuict doit de ceux etre aimee,
>> Qui souffrent en ce jour une peine eternelle.
>> Ostez-vous le desir de s'efforcer a celle
>> Qui libre veut mourir pour ne vivre captive?
>
> (I.254-57)

[An eternal night should be cherished by those who suffer an eternal pain in daylight. Are you preventing the last wish of a woman who prefers to die free rather than to live captive?]

Even Octavien rationalizes the cares of his office: "Jamais la terre en tout advantureuse / N'a sa personne entierement heureuse" (II.465-68) ("High estate, reckless in every respect, never leaves anyone completely happy"). In each case rhetoric takes the place of action. The audience needs less to reconstruct what led up to the present event than to weigh the characters' accounts of it and explore their implications. Jodelle's rhetorical strategies make that purpose clear.

The play's rhetorical action focuses on two traditional issues, the glory of kings and the downfall of lovers. Intertextually it uses time-worn aphorisms, epigrams, and moral sententiae as elocutionary devices for the political issue, and the dominant lyric forms of courtly French poetry for the amatory one.[10] Octavien's hollowness, sham, and manipulation of illusion emerge from the rhetoric of the first, and Cleopatre's confusion, emotional exhaustion, and luxuriant self-pity emerge from the second. In his confrontation with Cleopatre, Octavien embellishes his imperial authority with the verbal trappings of his office to demand for submission: "N'est-il pas clair que vous tachiez de faire / Par tous moyens Cesar vostre adversaire?" (III.533-34) ("Isn't it clear that you're trying in every possible way to make Caesar your adversary?"). Cleopatre, however, mocks him with the Petrarchan figures that she and Antoine had used earlier to claim love as the reason for her conduct, and at the same time she mocks herself by submitting to the debilitating implications of her own poetic language;

> Songe, Cesar, combien peult la puissance
> D'un traistre amour, mesme en sa jouissance:
> Et pense encor que mon foible courage
> N'eust pas souffert sans l'amoureuse rage.
>
> (III.549-52)

[Imagine, Caesar, how much the power of a treacherous love can accomplish even in its delight: and think, moreover, how my weak courage would not have failed if it hadn't been for amorous madness.]

Cleopatre's scorn for the official rhetoric of royal governance complements her servitude to a powerful amatory rhetoric. Their ironic juxtaposition brings the play to its climax in act IV during the heroine's obsequies at Antoine's tomb. With her classically balanced cadences, anaphorical repetitions, iterated apostrophes, and Petrarchan antitheses, she uses her dead beloved as an occasion for a patently rhetorical construction:

> Antoine, o cher Antoine, Antoine ma moitie,
> Ah Antoine n'eust eu des cieux l'inimitie,
> Antoine, Antoine, helas! dont le malheur me prive,
> Entens la foible voix d'une foible captive.
>
> (IV.1343-46)

[Antoine, o dear Antoine, Antoine my better half, ah Antoine, if only you hadn't met the hostility of heaven; Antoine, Antoine, alas, from whom misfortune separates me, hear the weak voice of a weak captive.]

Here is her tragedy. It radically modifies the tradition of Cleopatra as scheming queen and selfish lover. Jodelle's Cleopatre has surrendered her personal rhetorical voice to the demands both of her public role as queen and of her private one as a lover. She is captive not just to a political situation beyond her control. She is captive to a rhetoric of love whose force dominates all her utterances. Rhetoric has taken hold of her every statement so that neither as queen nor as lover can she react with straightforward simplicity.

The audience that Shakespeare created for his *Antony and Cleopatra* fifty-four years later had a cultural base discernibly broader than Jodelle's, but it was still called upon to devote its utmost attention to the text's rhetorical implications. Here, however, we may discern a shift from Jodelle's interest in modifying traditional problems of royal conduct to Shakespeare's interest in exploring more general problems of love, loyalty, and human relationships. Historically and sociologically the Elizabethan theater represented "a democratic institution in an intensely undemocratic age."[11] The unique composition of its members from all walks of life on both sides of the stage reflects this condition. The economics of the theater reflect it too. Distinguished from its academic and courtly counterparts on the Continent, it was a professional enterprise conducted by professional actors and businessmen attracting lucrative audiences. It performed regularly at public and private houses indoors and outdoors, in provinces and cities, for rich and poor, literate and illiterate.

Shakespeare's Globe Theater drew a largely plebian clientele that mingled with genteel patrons of the private theaters. By the time Shakespeare wrote *Antony and Cleopatra* in 1607, however, his company was regularly touring the provinces (especially during times of plague in the city, such as the winter of 1608–09), and was likewise performing before courtly audiences at palaces in and around London. In August 1608, moreover, his King's Men acquired lease of the private Blackfriar's Theater for indoor performances during the winter months. There it could expect more sophisticated audiences attuned to a finer literary and dramatic virtuosity, with perhaps a more academic awareness of literary tradition. *Antony and Cleopatra* premiered at the Globe, but the earliest text that we have of the play is the First Folio of 1623, and that text might not inconceivably incorporate some revisions for its later indoor audience.

Neither Elizabethan ethnology nor the text's theatrical history fully explains the audience's character, however. Shakespeare's rhetorical gestures toward identifying his audience with, and dissociating it from, the play's characters afford more evidence.[12] They involve the audience in a common pursuit that binds together noble and commoner, townsman and tradesman alike. Each of its members can participate in the play's verbal dialectic. Its requirements for admission are neither education nor background, though both certainly enhance its reception, but a keen ear and a quick wit.

The mercurial qualities demanded of Shakespeare's audience find their concrete textual analogy in the play's mercurial language. Rhymes, puns, assonances, and other verbal repetitions abound.[13] Their self-referentiality, their poetic conventions, their inter- and extratextual echoes all urge the audience in its collectivity and individuality to explore the tissue of the play as deeply as it can. Perhaps its best opportunities occur in the play's eight brief soliloquies. As privileged moments distributed throughout the text they offer the audience an important opportunity to examine its relationships with the characters. Just as the speakers of these soliloquies fabricate a variety of role-playing situations for themselves, so the audience must do the same thing for itself.[14] It must observe the protagonists' actions as a moral bystander and at the same time sympathize with them as an imaginative participant. It must go beyond the traditional accounts of their lives to seek more substantial grounds for their conduct, and it must find those grounds in both what they say and what they do. It must engage fully in the moral dialectic implied in the text.

The first two soliloquies reveal Antony's contradictory impulses both to renounce Cleopatra and to remain with her. "I must from this enchanting queen break off" (I.ii.125), he says after receiving news of Fulvia's death.[15] In a later soliloquy he agrees to a truce with Octavius by marrying Octavia, but he resolves nonetheless to rejoin Cleopatra in Egypt: "Though I make this marriage for my peace, / I' the east my pleasure lies" (II.iii.38–39). The contrast between the two soliloquies allows the audience to view Antony from a double perspective. The first displays the Roman Antony who sees himself very much as Philo saw him in the play's first lines. He enumerates his roles as the husband, now widower of Fulvia; as philanderer with Cleopatra; as repentant of his behavior and wishful about the past ("The hand could pluck her back that shov'd her on," [I.ii.124]); as resentful of his servitude to the "enchanting queen"; and as one who must now rouse himself from idleness and dotage to resume his proper role as Roman commander. The second soliloquy displays the Egyptian Antony who sees himself as Cleopatra sees him. After the scene at Rome with the cunning Octavius and drunken Lepidus, the recall to Egypt seems all the more inviting. Antony recognizes that he's been manipulated into marrying Octavia for political reasons, and that whatever the odds, Octavius is bound to triumph: the latter's "quails ever / Beat mine, inhoop'd, at odds" (II.iii.36–37). The rhetorical strategies here reinforce the contrast. Antony's speech in the first soliloquy is Roman, laconic, devoid of figures; here it is rich, luxuriant, evoking the fullness of its speaker even in his apparent inferiority to Octavius.

The audience partakes of similarly privileged moments in Enobarbus's two soliloquies that follow. Antony's contradictory impulses begin to affect the behavior of others. Enobarbus now weighs his own opposing decisions first to leave Antony—"I will seek /Some way to leave him" (III.xiii.200–201)—and then to punish himself for having betrayed Antony—"I am alone the villain of the earth, / And feel I am so most" (IV.vi.30–31). Just as with Antony's soliloquies, Enobarbus's develop a private tone that commands attention. The plain speech of the first soliloquy makes his commentary on Antony's action all the more compelling as an alternative point of view. It invites the audience explicitly to articulate its own moral response to Antony's behavior. When Enobarbus emphasizes "A diminution in our captain's brain" (III.xiii.198), he has valid grounds for scorning Antony. The second soliloquy, however, addresses Antony in more elaborate figures as a "mine of bounty . . . / . . . when my turpitude / Thou dost crown with gold" (IV.vi.32-34). Here the speaker confesses himself an inadequate judge of Antony's character, and with him the audience ought to explore its own inadequacy. Antony's moral worth has begun to confound received opinion. Nor does the audience find that Enobarbus is alone in expressing confusion. Scarus also does it in a brief soliloquy just before Antony embarks upon his course of self-destruction: "Antony / Is valiant, and dejected, and by starts / His fretted fortunes give him hope and fear" (IV.xii.6-8). Here, moreover, the text radically alters the traditional view by representing Antony in this ambivalent frame of mind after as well as before the battle of Actium. The audience by now realizes that no action in this play is decisive, except death.

Antony's two ensuing soliloquies show his resolve toward that decisive action. In them he reveals an unprecedented firmness of purpose. Both refer to the hero's forebears in classical myth, and they presume the audience's awareness of the roles of those traditional archetypes. The first is an apostrophe to Hercules, Antony's mythic ancestor: "The shirt of Nessus is upon me, teach me, /Alcides, thou mine ancestor, thy rage" (IV.xii.43-44). Hercules's rage at Lichas for investing him with the poisoned shirt impels the audience to compare it with Antony's rage at Cleopatra for her alleged betrayal of him at Alexandria. Rather than denigrate Cleopatra, however, the soliloquy directs the audience's attention to Antony's own inner magnitude. It is important to catch the shift in perspective registered by the movement from the third to the first person pronoun. Following Hercules' cue in the mythic paradigm Antony will "with those hands that grasp'd the heaviest club, / Subdue my worthiest self" (IV.xii.46-47). Though he vows "the witch shall die," he emphasizes most strongly his own Herculean potential for self-destruction. For the participating audience, then, the soliloquy suggests how Antony's suicide results from his role-playing. In his search for a better role to express his selfhood, Antony chooses the model of Hercules even if it ironically entails doing away with himself.

Antony's next soliloquy confirms this interaction between role and self barely fifty lines later. Here again Antony testifies to his love for Cleopatra. He has just told Eros that his mistress's betrayal has robbed him of his selfhood: "Here I am Antony, /Yet cannot hold this visible shape" (IV.xiv.13–14). Now the audience shares his private thoughts as he plans his death. Misled by the false report of her death as proof of her innocence, he offers his own as proof of his repentance: "I will o'ertake thee, Cleopatra, and / Weep for my pardon" (IV.xiv.44–45). Continuing his address to her, he envisions their reunion in the afterlife in a reference that presumes the audience's understanding:

> Where souls do couch on flowers, we'll hand in hand,
> And with our sprightly port make the ghosts gaze:
> Dido, and her Aeneas, shall want troops,
> And all the haunt be ours.
>
> (IV.xiv.51–54)

Once more he mythifies his experience, but with a strange inversion of traditional roles that upsets the audience's expectations. He represents Dido's faith as unquestioned, even though Aeneas had betrayed her for a higher purpose. His own faith in Cleopatra, however, has been severely tested. She has betrayed him for baser purposes, whether real or imagined. Antony tries to repair the breach in the myth by depicting Dido's reunion with Aeneas in Hades. This reunion, of course, runs counter to their separation in the *Aeneid*. For his own breach with Cleopatra, moreover, Antony can only project an imaginative resolution through words. He invents a role for himself to play, not so much in conformity with the Plutarchan tradition as with the dramatic possibilities of the role–playing implied in Shakespeare's own text. The audience comes finally to see Antony as an actor staging his own performance, in command of himself and of his love for Cleopatra.

The play's final soliloquy is Cleopatra's. It is her only soliloquy and the play's shortest one, yet it proves decisive in manipulating the audience's sympathies in her favor.[16] It extends Antony's rhetorical mode by representing in subdued metonomy Cleopatra's firm resolve to die. "My resolution's plac'd, and I have nothing / Of woman in me" (V.ii.237–38). Her resolution affords the audience the best possible counterweight to a faulty understanding of the play. Cleopatra had foreseen the possibility of such a misunderstanding a few lines earlier in her remarks to Iras about what awaits her in Rome: "The quick comedians / Ex-temporally will stage us, and present / Our Alexandrian revels" (V.ii.215–17).[17] In a good performance Antony should not "be brought drunken forth" (218), nor should the boy–actor who plays Cleopatra squeak "i" the posture of a whore" (220). With their references to the staging of spectacles, the breaking of dramatic illusion, and the employment of boy actors, these lines evoke conditions of Elizabethan dramaturgy external to the action of the play. They prepare the audience for the heroine's final deed that puts the play's internal dynamics into proper perspective. Doubling in on itself, Shakespeare's verse manipulates the audience to question its own reception of the play. Its assigned role is to bear witness to an event of tragic magnitude. If it views the play as just another historical revel, then it has missed the point entirely.

Shakespeare's rhetorical strategies demand a particularly attentive audience. Like Jodelle's it must be willing to adjust its collective sights to the focus of a single poetic vision. The chief difference is that Jodelle appeals exclusively to an educated, aristocratic class. Shakespeare appeals to a wider group. Its common denominator is not class or rank but intelligence and sensitivity. This denominator faces the test of the play's soliloquy with sensitivity to the poetic rhythms as well as an awareness of its tradition. Though none of the soliloquies is longer than twenty-two lines (Antony's at IV.xii.18-49 is in fact cut in two by Cleopatra's intrusion at ll.30-39), while the shortest is only six lines (Cleopatra's at V.ii.235-40), taken as a group they epitomize the play's dense textuality. Shakespeare's audience must be clear-minded, subtle, and capacious to accommodate all its nuances.

Lohenstein's audience fifty-four years later is different from both Jodelle's and Shakespeare's. Its historical constituents were bourgeois, securely moneyed, politically powerful, socially influential. This audience has an interest in clearly defined moral problems with unambiguous outcomes. The play's themes reward its audience's interest even if they juxtapose contrary virtues and vices in a startling order. Its members must be inclined to take the play's shifting moral tones at their face values. Each of these values appeals to a different segment of the audience—young, old, male, female, bourgeois, noble. Accordingly the play addresses a variety of audiences in a variety of ways.

The first performance of Lohenstein's *Cleopatra* took place in Breslau, February 1661, at the prestigious Elisabethanum Gymnasium, acted by students at the school.[18] The audience's social composition doubtless included the students' bourgeois families, the school's educated faculty, occasional noble patrons from the court, and perhaps other prominent townsfolk. Subsequent performances may have taken place at various courts or in various towns, but the conditions of presentation do not change the roles assigned to the audience. And, though Lohenstein imparted substantial revisions to the play nearly twenty years later, he still retained the play's essentially sententious modality in his version of 1680.

Cleopatra's moral transformation from lusty mistress to scheming manipulator occurs in III.i. As she here prepares for her mock suicide, she hopes that Antonius will take his own life so she can survive in Augustus' reign. For her plan to work, however, she needs an audience who will report the event to her paramour. She summons her ladies to act as witnesses: "Diss Schauspiel muss in sich was mehr Personen schlussen" (III.i.61) ("This drama must include more characters").[19] Her play-acting amounts to *Schauspiel* in more than one dramatic sense. The ladies-in-waiting seek to persuade her against suicide with conventional arguments. Cleopatra rejects their pleas with a volley of stoic *sententiae* drawn from countless Renaissance and Baroque commonplace books. If the silkworm weaves its own grave, why shouldn't she? "Pflagt nicht der Seiden-Wurm ihm selbst sein Grab zu weben?" (III.i.90). Beauty is as smoke; youth a shadow: "Die Schonheit ist ein Rauch / die Jugend ist ein Schatten" (III.i.106). Fate rules all our actions anyway: "So libkost auch das Gluck uns / wenns uns wil vergraben" (III.i.121). It is better to die a noble death than to live a thousand years: "Ein ruhmlich Todt ist mehr / Als tausend Jahre wehrt" (1661 version only: III.i.127-28). In voice and address her argument is full of cliches that underscore the weakness of her play-acting. Cleopatra is not sincere, nor is her rhetoric.[20]

Cleopatra's *Schauspiel* takes a more dramatic rhetorical turn when she bids her ladies help her to prepare for death.

> Setzt mir nicht ferner zu mit den unfruchtbarn Thranen!
> Helfft mir vielmehr den Weg in diesen Garten bahnen
> Da ich mein Leben kan der Nachwelt pfropfen ein.
>   (III.i.57-59)

[Deter me no further with fruitless tears! Help me instead to prepare my way to this garden, where I can engraft my life onto the afterlife.]

Tropologically her requests evoke a host of funereal traditions from ancient literature. Cleopatra is playing to the hilt her false role as suicide; she is posing as a classical heroine seeking a classical death. The sheer rhetorical ingenuity of her speech indicates her ability to manipulate words, actions, and audiences. This Cleopatra enjoys her *Schauspiel* because it ensures her control over the world around her.

A second *Schauspiel* in IV.ii affords a greater dramatic irony. After acknowledging Augustus as victor over herself and Antonius and consigning her kingdom to him, Cleopatra confesses her love for him in a calculated gesture of play-acting. In him she says she sees the image of his uncle, Julius Caesar, and she feels the flames of her old love rise again; what she hopes to achieve is Augustus' support and protection: "Ich brenn'! ich brenn'! August! denn durch des Keysers Glider / Zeigt sich mein Julius / mein Julius sich wieder" (IV.i.528-29) ("I am burning, I am burning, Augustus, for in your majesty's own body my Julius, my Julius appears once more before me"). Augustus proceeds to play with her in courtly fashion, dubbing her "Du Venus unser Zeit / du Sonne dieser Welt" (IV.i.583) ("You Venus of our time, you sun of this world"), and surrendering to her charms: "August ergibt sich dir / er lagt die Lorberkrantze / Fur deinen Myrten ab" (IV.i.585-86) ("Augustus surrenders to you; he renounces the laurel crowns for your myrtles"). All along he has wanted to bring Cleopatra to Rome in triumph, to assign her a role in his own *Schauspiel* signaling military victory over all his rivals. "Dass ihrer Hochmuth Strahl der Romer Schau-spiel sei" (1661 version only: IV.i.216) ("so that your display of pride might become a spectacle for the Romans"). All along she has resisted this humiliation. Now Augustus skillfully turns her own amatory rhetoric back on her. Cleopatra sees through the maneuver, however. Augustus' rhetorical references to conventional love poetry score as much success with her as her own rhetorical references to classical funereal poetry scored in her mock-death scene. She has hidden her sham in the discursive space of other texts and now she recognizes that Augustus is doing the same thing. The rhetorical situation functions as a straightforward index to both characters' Machiavellian manipulations.[21]

Lohenstein's Cleopatra is a lover enraged, a queen unsure of herself, a cunning politician outwitted by a superior politician. The shift of gravity from the representation of her as a wanton lover in the early acts to that of her as a political intriguer in the later acts indicates the breadth of the play's moral boundaries and the scope of the audience's interests.[22] The play encompasses several actions and appeals to several fictive audiences. First it throughout offers a range of generalized Senecan *sententiae* that appeal to bourgeois espousals of conventional middle-class values. Next it presents *topoi* from classical poetry in specific scenes, particularly through references to Vergil, Ovid, and Horace that self-consciously appeal to newly educated classes. But third it embodies a few faint traces of more recent European amatory poetry, mainly through references to Guarini and Marino in the first half of the play, that appeal more widely to contemporaneous literary fashion. Fourth, it dramatizes the theme of political intrigue in the second half of the play with particular relevance for the ruling classes in the audience. Finally, it evokes details of ancient history more elaborately than earlier plays for particular interest to the academic sector and the student audience. Lohenstein's problem is to keep these audiences in touch with each other and with the play. He does not always succeed; or, at least, he doesn't always establish as much harmony among them as Jodelle, Shakespeare, and other Renaissance dramatists had done. The bourgeois and the aristocratic elements fit together in an uneasy combination. It is a mistake, I think, to try to see Lohenstein's audience as a homogeneous whole. Historical distance tends to efface distinctions among registers of audience. An awareness of the intertextual resonances, on the other hand, helps to reassert those distinctions and to imply in their variety and multiplicity a varied and multiple audience.

The distance from Lohenstein's play back to Shakespeare's is much greater than from Shakespeare's back to Jodelle's, even though an equivalent span of fifty-four years separates each. The reason for the distance lies partly in the concept of character. Jodelle's play is a tragedy of fortune that its characters have no power to oppose or resist. The false report of Cleopatre's death does not lure Antoine to suicide; instead he kills himself in desperation over Octavien's refusal to do single combat with him: "tant que malheureuse i'vse / Du malheureux remede" (I.136–37) ("Unfortunate, I try an unfortunate remedy"). Shakespeare's play, on the other hand, suggests more complicated motives. Cleopatra issues her false report at Charmian's suggestion partly to punish Antony for his accusing her of conspiring with Caesar and partly to test his love for her: "Hence, Mardian, / And bring me how he takes my death" (IV.xiii.8–9). In Lohenstein, however, Cleopatra has become a figure of treachery. She deliberately incites Antonius to suicide because only by eliminating him can she sue for protection from the stronger Octavius.

This movement from misfortune to ambiguity to outright treachery in the heroine's motivations may clarify some aspects of literary history's passage from Renaissance to Baroque. Viewed seriatim, however, it fails to explain the oblique ways in which literary history develops. Its movement does not follow a continuous linear progression from one point to another, especially when the departure seems relatively simple and uncomplicated, the transition mature and fully developed, and the end strained and exhausted. Shakespeare's play towers over Jodelle's and Lohenstein's in dramaturgical and poetic complexity, but not just because it reflects differences in the author's relative ages and sociological backgrounds. The concept of different audiences provides a much better index to literary history.

The choral interludes of Jodelle's and Lohenstein's plays by themselves indicate the kinds of audience that the plays address.[23] Whereas

Renaissance choruses like Jodelle's address a single audience, Lohenstein's manifest a diversity that calls for several audiences. The interludes (*Reyen*) of Lohenstein's play underscores the expansion of its central action. They import into the play several plays–within–the–play. Thus the interlude of act I pits the goddess Fortuna against Jupiter, Neptune, Pluto, and their attendant deities, while the interlude of act V shows the rivers Nile and Tiber prophesying that the Danube and Rhine will one day host the Holy Roman Empire. In contrast to the mythic mode of these interludes, the ones in acts II and IV unfold in the pastoral mode, the first in the ancient world of Paris's judgment of Venus over Juno and Pallas, the second in the world of the play's action among shepherds and shepherdesses who prefer the simple life to the world's riches. The interlude of act III occurs in a lyric space outside time and human action, and records a dialogue among Clotho, Lachesis, and Atropos on the fate of Antonius and Cleopatra.

This expansion of generic, modal, and stylistic possibilities in Lohenstein's *Reyen* of course implicates various audiences capable of receiving and discriminating among the genres, modes, and styles incorporated. By contrast, Jodelle's choruses with the consistent style of their lyric embellishments (as in the rose simile, I.133) and mythic comparisons (as with the Giants, Prometheus, and Icarus, II.700) and the coherent vision of their sympathy with Cleopatre (IV.1325), fear for her future (IV.1427), and sorrow over her death (V.1591), appeal to a homogeneous audience. They represent a deliberate contraction of generic, modal, and stylistic possibilities better to circumscribe its audience's attitudes and expectations. In Shakespeare's play the poetic patterns of imagery implicit in the characters' soliloquies serve the same purpose. This rhetorical contraction is typical of Renaissance texts. Rhetorical expansion like Lohenstein's, however, can occur only when the audience rests secure in its familiarity with each of the rhetorical possibilities. It occurs when Renaissance genres, modes, and styles have developed to the point of wide acceptance among audiences and can thenceforth enter into combination with each other. This combinatory process characterizes the Baroque period.

Literary history, then, entails much more than a set of references to texts and traditions. It entails as well a concretization of attitudes between authors and audiences based on their experiences of and expectations about those texts and traditions. Using the audience's role as a norm to assess the author's, we can come to certain conclusions about the development of literary history. What we can discern is the splintering, fragmentation, dispersal, and general problematization of the audience's attitudes in the passage from Renaissance to Baroque.

Changes in the rhetorical situation of each text's fictive audience can show how a tradition develops through the audience's understanding of past texts and its application of that understanding to new ones. They can show how possibilities for repetition with a difference emerge when the audience questions each text's areas of indeterminacy. They can point to modal and stylistic distinctions between texts belonging to the same genre, and to ways that literary history moves in different directions on modal, stylistic, and generic levels at unequal rates of speed. In asking how the audience's roles provide evidence for understanding the literary past, we might well discover some of the forms and patterns that characterize it. In this regard the motifs of Cleopatra in Jodelle, Shakespeare, and Lohenstein can serve as an exemplary model.

Cornell University

NOTES

1. See William J. Kennedy, *Rhetorical Norms in Renaissance Literature* (New Haven: Yale University Press, 1978), pp. 3–19, 190–91.

2. Hans George Gadamer, *Truth and Method* (New York: Seabury Press, 1975), pp. 258–64.

3. For the concept of concretization see Roman Ingarden, *The Literary Work of Art,* trans. George Grabowicz (Evanston, Illinois: Northwestern University Press, 1971), pp. 332–55. See also Jan Mukarovsky, "The Individual and Literary Development," in *The Word and Verbal Art,* trans. and ed. John Burbank and Peter Steiner (New Haven: Yale University Press, 1977), pp. 161–79, and "The Whole in the Theory of Art," in *Structure, Sign, and Function,* trans. and ed. John Burbank and Peter Steiner (New Haven: Yale University Press, 1978), pp. 70–81; and Juri Lotman, *La structure du texte artistique,* trans. Anne Fournier et al. (Paris: Gallimard, 1973).

4. Walter Ong, S.J., *Interfaces of the Word* (Ithaca: Cornell University Press, 1977), pp. 53–81. For the concept of the fictive audience see also Lowry Nelson, Jr., "The Fictive Reader and Literary Self-Reflexiveness," in *The Disciplines of Criticism,* ed. Thomas M. Greene (New Haven: Yale University Press, 1968), pp. 173–92; and Kennedy, *Rhetorical Norms,* esp. pp. 5–7.

5. See Alan Wardman, *Plutarch's Lives* (Berkeley and Los Angeles: University of California Press, 1974). For the translation of Plutarch into Latin see John Edwin Sandys, *A History of Classical Scholarship,* 3 vols. (Cambridge: Cambridge University Press, 1908). For texts available to Jodelle, see Lowell Bryce Ellis's introduction to *Cleopatre Captive* (Philadelphia: University of Pennsylvania Series in The Romance Languages and Literatures, 1946). For an excellent general survey of the traditions available to the Elizabethans see Janet Adelman's superb study of Shakespeare's play, *The Common Liar* (New Haven: Yale University Press, 1973). See also Herbert Rothschild, "The Oblique Encounter: Shakespeare's Confrontation of Plutarch," *English Literary Renaissance,* 6 (1976), 404–29. An exhaustive survey of Renaissance and Baroque plays on

Cleopatra is G. H. Moeller, *Die Auffassung der Cleopatra in der Tragodiendichtung der romanischgermanischen Nationen* (Freiburg: Universitatsverlag, 1888).

6. See Felix Vodicka, "Die Konkretisation des literarischen Werks," in *Die Struktur der literarischen Entwicklung,* ed. Jurij Striedter (Munich: Wilhelm Fink, 1976), pp. 87-125; Hans Gunther, "Grundbegriffe der Rezeptions—und Wirkungsanalyse," *Poetica* 4 (1971), 224-43, and Herta Schmid, "Zum Begriff der asthetischen Konkretisation," *Sprache im technischen Zeitalter* 36 (1970), 290-318. For more recent extensions of the socio-historical context in literary theory see Peter Hohendahl, "Introduction to Reception Aesthetics," *New German Critique* 10 (1977), 29-63, and "Prolegomena to a History of Literary Criticism," *New German Critique* 11 (1977), 151-63.

7. For a subtle study of how author and audience—especially the play's first intended audience, Henri II—are themselves represented with the play's language, see Georg R. Garner, "Tragedy, Sovereignty, and the Sign: Jodelle's *Cleopatre Captive*" *Canadian Review of Comparative Literature* 5 (1978), 245-79. For the characters' tragic entrapment in their own language see Timothy Reiss, "*Cleopatre* and the Enchanted Circle," in *Image and Symbol in the Renaissance,* ed. Andre Winandy, *Yale French Studies* 47 (1972), 199-210.

8. For "rhetoric's hold over humanist practice, creating a fundamental distinction between sixteenth-century and Classical tragedy," see Donald Stone, Jr., *French Humanist Tragedy* (Manchester: Manchester University Press, 1974), pp. 156 ff.; and for "the distinct difference in the kind of responses demanded of the spectator, even over the relatively short period between 1600 and 1640 or so," see T. J. Reiss, *Toward Dramatic Illusion* (New Haven: Yale University Press, 1971), p. 2 and passim.

9. Quotations are from Estienne Jodelle, *Cleopatre Captive,* ed. Lowell Bryce Ellis (Philadelphia: University of Pennsylvania Series in the Romance Languages and Literatures, 1946). I have modernized "i," "j," "u," and "v" in this edition.

10. Though Jodelle's talent in the lyric was meager, he still adapted lyric forms and motifs for his own purposes; see Emile Faguet, *La Tragedie francaise au XVI[e] siecle* (1912; rpt. Geneva: Sklatine Reprint, 1969), p. 86; for his Pleiade emphasis on literary glory see Raymond Lebegue, *La Tragedie francaise de la Renaissance* (Paris: Societe d'Edition d'Enseignement Superieur, 1954), p. 34.

11. Alfred Harbage, *Shakespeare's Audience* (New York: Columbia University Press, 1941), p. 11. For a thorough study of the character of the English economy that produced such aesthetic conditions, see Robert Weimann, *Drama und Wirklichkeit in der Shakespearezeit* (Halle: Max Niemeyer, 1958), pp. 146 f. and 156-60. Among the myriad studies of Elizabethan playhouses, one may consult the basic works of E. K. Chambers, A. M. Nagler, Andrew Gurr, and Glynne Wickham. For specific commentary on how practices in the private theaters may have affected Shakespeare's production, see Alfred Harbage, *Shakespeare and the Rival Traditions* (New York: Barnes and Noble, 1952).

12. For the audience's identification and dissociation with the characters see Albert Cook, *Shakespeare's Enactment* (Chicago: The Swallow Press, 1976); see also Herbert Lindenberger's emphasis on how "the growth process does not take place so much within the characters of the play as in our own consciousness," *Historical Drama* (Chicago: University of Chicago Press, 1975), p. 144.

13. For acute study of the language of the play see Maurice Charney, *Shakespeare's Roman Plays* (Cambridge, Mass.: Harvard University Press, 1961), pp. 11 ff.; Sigurd Burckhardt, *Shakespearean Meanings* (Princeton: Princeton University Press, 1968), pp. 279-84; and Rosalie Colie's contrast between the Attic and Asiatic styles in *Shakespeare's Living Art* (Princeton: Princeton University Press, 1974), pp. 168-207. For a stimulating

study of the audience's role in evaluating the rhetorical styles, see Joel B. Altman, *The Tudor Play of Mind* (Berkeley and Los Angeles: University of California Press, 1978).

14. The most complete study of Shakespearean roles is Thomas Van Laan, *Role-playing in Shakespeare* (Toronto: University of Toronto Press, 1978), esp. pp. 215-22. On *Antony and Cleopatra* the best study of its role-playing is David Daiches, "Imagery and Meaning in *Antony and Cleopatra,*" *English Studies* 43 (1962), 343-58.

15. Quotations are from William Shakespeare, *Antony and Cleopatra,* the Arden edition, ed. M. R. Ridley (Cambridge, Mass.: Harvard University Press, 1954).

16. For typically divergent interpretations of Cleopatra's intentions in this scene, see Derek Traversi, *Shakespeare: The Roman Plays* (London: Hollis and Carter, 1963), pp. 147, 196 ff.; A. P. Riemer, *A Reading of Shakespeare's "Antony and Cleopatra"* (Sydney: Sydney University Press, 1968), pp. 9, 77 ff.; Philip Traci, *The Love Play of "Antony and Cleopatra"* (The Hague: Mouton, 1980), pp. 58 ff.; Kenneth Muir, *Shakespeare's Tragic Sequence* (London: Hutchinson University Library, 1972), pp. 156-71; and Charles Hallett, "Aspects of the Sublunary World in *Antony and Cleopatra,*" *Journal of English and Germanic Philology* 75 (1976), 75-89.

17. See the fine analysis of these lines in Phyllis Rackin, "Shakespeare's Boy Cleopatra, the Decorum of Nature, and the Golden World of Poetry," *PMLA* 87 (1972), 201-12; and by Julian Markels, *The Pillar of the World* (Columbus: Ohio State University Press, 1968), pp. 3 ff.

18. See the exhaustive study of the sociology of Lohenstein's audience and its horizons of expectation in Alberto Martino, *Daniel Casper von Lohenstein: Storia della sua ricezione* (Pisa: Athenaeum, 1975); Martino emphasizes "l'omogeneita culturale e spirituale che sussiste fra autore e pubblico," p. 191; I concur below with the sociological conclusion, but contest the literary one when I argue for the multiplicity of the audience's expectations and attitudes.

19. This line appears only in the edition of 1661, ed. Ilse-Marie Barth (Stuttgart: Philipp Reclam, 1965); except where I have noted otherwise, however, I have quoted from the text of 1680 edited by K. G. Just, *Afrikanische Trauerspiele* (Stuttgart: Anton Hiersemann, 1957). For a complete comparison of the first version with the second, see Joerg C. Juretzka, *Zur Dramatik Daniel Caspers von Lohenstein* (Meisenheim am Glan: Anton Hain, 1976), pp. 38-62.

20. For Lohenstein's preoccupation with "die Rollenhaftigkeit des Menschentums," see Fritz Schaufelberger, *Das Tragische in Lohensteins Trauerspielen* (Leipzig: Huber, 1945), pp. 116-18; for the appeal to fate see Gerhard Spellenberg, *Verhangnis und Geschichte* (Bad Homburg: Gehlen, 1970), pp. 155-57; for a review of modern criticism see Bernhard Asmuth, *Daniel Casper von Lohenstein* (Stuttgart: Metzler, 1971), pp. 27-31.

21. See the interpretation of Klaus Gunther Just, *Die Trauerspiele Lohensteins* (Berlin: Erich Schmidt, 1961), pp. 155-61, challenged by Gerald Gillespie, *Lohenstein's Historical Tragedies* (Columbus: Ohio State University Press, 1965), pp. 81-110.

22. See the conception of the contemporary court as "der innerste Schauplatz" in Walter Benjamin, *Ursprung des deutchen Trauerspiels* (Frankfurt am Main: Suhrkamp, 1963), pp. 90-98.

23. For close analysis of the *Reyen* in this play see Juretzka, *Lohenstein,* pp. 104-23; for their functions in other plays see Eric Lunding, *Das Schlesische Kunstdrama* (Copenhagen: P. Hassa, 1940), pp. 106 ff., and Ulrich Fulleborn, *Die barocke Grundspannung Zeit*-Ewigkeit in den Trauerspielen Lohensteins (Stuttgart: Metzler, 1969), pp. 37-40.

The Bottom Translation

Jan Kott

> "Bless thee, Bottom, bless thee! Thou art translated."
> — *A Midsummer Night's Dream,* III.i.113

"*L*ove looks not with the eyes, but with the mind" (I.i.234).[1]
This soliloquy of Helena is part of a discourse on love and
madness. Does desire also look with "the mind," and not with "the
eyes"? Titania awakens from her dream, looks at the monster, and
desires him. When Lysander and Demetrius awaken, they see only a
girl's body, and desire it. Is desire "blind" and love "seeing"? Or is
love "blind" and desire "seeing"? "And therefore is wing'd Cupid
painted blind" (I.i.235). Puck is the culprit in *A Midsummer Night's
Dream,* for he awakens a desire by spraying love potion in the eyes of
the sleeping lovers. In the poetic discourse of *A Midsummer Night's
Dream,* "blind Cupid" is the agent of love. Are Puck and Cupid
exchangeable?

Helena's soliloquy is recited by a young actress or, as in Elizabethan
theater, by a boy acting the woman's part. The soliloquy is the *voice* of
the actor. But it is not, or not only, the voice of the *character.* It is a part
of a polyphonic, or many-*voiced,* discourse on love. In *A Midsummer
Night's Dream* this discourse is more than the poetic commentary to the
events taking place on stage. And the action on stage is more than
illustration of the text. The discourse and the action not only comple-
ment each other but also appear to contradict each other. The dramatic
tension and the intellectual richness result from this confrontation of
discourse and action.

The same similes and icons recur from the first to the last act of the
play. *Icon* may be the most appropriate term here, for Cupid is the most
significant image in this discourse. This "child" (I.i.238), "the boy
Love" (241), waggish, foreswearing, and beguiling, repeats the post-
classical icon of the blind or blindfolded Cupid.

From the early medieval poem, "I am blind and I make blind," to

117

Erasmus' *The Praise of Folly,* the icon is constant: "But why is Cupide alwaies lyke a yonge boie? why? but that he is a trifler, neither doyng, nor thynkyng any wyse acte" (21.20).[2] But this blind or blindfolded Cupid, associated in the Middle Ages with allegories of evil and darkness—Death, Synagogue, Night, Infidelity, and Blind Fortune— became by the Renaissance a sign with two opposing values and semantic opposition. "Blind" Cupid is a "seeing" one, but now seeing, as in Pico della Mirandola, "with an incorporeal eye."[3] This second Cupid, blind but seeing "with the mind," appears soon after the first within Helena's soliloquy:

> Things base and vile, holding no quantity,
> Love can transpose to form and dignity
> (I.i.232–33).

Who and what is spoken of? Hermia, who is "sweet" and "fair," is hardly "base and vile." Helena does not know yet that Hermia is soon to be her rival. The "real" Helena, a character in the comedy, cannot be here referring to Hermia. The *voice* of the actor speaking of the madness of Eros forecasts Titania's infatuation with the "monster." But not only Bottom was "translated" that night. Both couples of young lovers were also "translated": "Am I not Hermia? Are you not Lysander?" (III. ii.273). Bottom's metamorphosis is only the climax of the events in the forests. This "night–rule" (III.ii.5) ends immediately after Bottom's return to human shape. Oberon and Titania "vanish." Theseus and Hippolyta return with the beginning of the new day in place of their night doubles. The lovers wake up from their "dream." And Bottom too wakes up from his:

> I have had a dream, past the wit of man to say what dream it was. Man is but an ass if he go about to expound this dream. . . . The eye of man hath not heard, the ear of man hath not seen, man's hand is not able to taste, his tongue to conceive, nor his heart to report, what my dream was (IV.i.204–06, 209–12).

The source of these astonishing lines is now well known. "It must be accepted," wrote Frank Kermode in his *Early Shakespeare* (1961), "that this is a parody of 1 Corinthians 2.9–10":

> Eye hath not seen, nor ear heard, neither have entered into the heart of man the things which God hath prepared for them that love him. But God hath revealed *them* unto us by his Spirit: for the Spirit searcheth all things, yea, the deep things of God.

Kermode quoted the King James Version. In Tyndale (1534) and in the Geneva New Testament (1557) the last verse reads: "the spirite searcheth all thinges, ye the bottome of Goddes secrets."[4] The "Athenian" weaver probably inherited his name from Paul's letter in old translations. The spirit which reaches to "the bottome" of all mysteries haunts Bottom. But just "translated" into an ass, Bottom translates Paul in his own way: "I will get Peter Quince to write a ballad of this dream: it shall be called 'Bottom's Dream,' because it hath no bottom" (IV.i.212–15).

But Bottom was not the only one in *A Midsummer Night's Dream* to read Corinthians. We find another echo of Paul's letter in Helena's soliloquy:

> Things base and vile, holding no quantity,
> Love can transpose to form and dignity

Paul had written: "And base things of the world, and things which are despised, hath God chosen, *yea,* and things which are not to bring to naught things that are" (1 Cor. 1.28). In Tyndale and in the Geneva Bible this verse starts: "and vile thinges of the worlde." "Things base" in Helena's lines, appears to be borrowed from the Geneva Bible, and "vile" repeats the wording of the Authorized Version.

The final aim of philological criticism is to establish the relations between texts and their principal sources. Interpretation starts where philological criticism ends. The term "text" does not have the same meaning in philology and in hermeneutics.[5] For an interpreter a "text" does not exist independently of its readings. Great texts, and perhaps even more so quotations from great texts, literal or parodistic, form together with their readings, a literary and cultural tradition. They become overgrown with commentaries and *lectiae*. Interpretations and commentaries become a part of their life. Great texts and quotations continuously repeated are *active* in intellectual radiation which gives them new meaning and changes old ones. Great texts converse among themselves. But borrowings and quotations are never neutral. Each quotation enlists its own context to challenge the author's text for better understanding or for mockery.

The verse from Corinthians parodied by Bottom and the biblical "things base and vile" in Helena's lines refer to Bottom's transformation and to Titania's sudden infatuation with the monster—both borrowed from Apuleius' *The Golden Ass*. Shakespeare might have read Apuleius in Latin or in Adlington's translation of 1566.[6] The riddle of *A Midsummer Night's Dream* is not only why Paul or Apuleius were evoked in it but also why *both* were evoked and involved in the dramatic nexus of Bottom's metamorphosis.

Both texts, Corinthians and *The Golden Ass,* were widely known, discussed, and quoted during the Renaissance. From the early sixteenth century until the late seventeenth century, both texts were read in two distinctly separate intellectual traditions having two discrete circuits, and interpreted in two *codes* which were complementary but contradictory. The first of these codes, which is simultaneously a tradition, a system of interpretation, and a "language," can be called Neoplatonic or hermetic. The second is the code of the carnival, or, more precisely, in Mikhail Bakhtin's terms, the tradition of *serio ludere:* the carnivalesque literature.[7]

> The carnival attitude possesses an indestructible vivacity and the mighty, life–giving power to transform. . . . For the first time in ancient literature the object of a *serious* (though at the same time comical) representation is presented without epical or tragical distance, presented not in the absolute past of myth and legend, but on the contemporary level, in direct and even crudely familiar contact with living contemporaries. In these genres mythical heroes and historical figures out of the past are deliberately and emphatically contemporized. . . .
>
> The serio–comical genres are not based on *legend* and do not elucidate themselves by means of the legend—they are *consciously* based on *experience* and on *free imagination;* their relationship to legend is in most cases deeply critical, and at times bears the cynical nature of the expose. . . . They reject the stylistic unity. . . . For them multiplicity of tone in a story and a mixture of the high and low, the serious and the comic, are typical: they made wide use . . . of parodically reconstructed quotations. In some of these genres the mixture of prose and poetic speech is observed, living dialects and slang are introduced, and various authorial masks appear.[8]

II

Paul's letter to the Corinthians is often invoked in the writings of Neoplatonists. In Mirandola, Ficino, Leone Ebreo, and Bruno, Paul can be found next to the Sibil of the *Aeneid,* King David, Orpheus, Moses, or Plato. For the hermetics and Florentine philosophers, as for Levi-Strauss, "myths rethink each other in a certain manner" ("d'une certaine manière, les mythes se pensent entre eux").[9] While icons and signifiers are borrowed from Plato and Plotinus, Heraclitus and Diony-sius Areopagite, the Psalms, Orphic hymns and cabalistic writings, the signified is always one and the same: the One beyond Being, unity in plurality, the God concealed. At times the method of the Neoplatonists resembles strangely the belief of poststructuralism and the new her-meneutics—that the permutation of signs, the inversion of their value and exchanges performed according to the rules of symbolic logic will, like the philosopher's stone, uncover the deep structure of Being and of the mind.

The blind Cupid of desire, the emblem of Elizabethan brothels, unveiled divine mysteries to Ficino and Mirandola. The "things base and vile" signify in this new Platonic code the "bottome of Goddes secretes." "Man," wrote Ficino, "ascends to the higher realms without discarding the lower world, and can descend to the lower world without foresaking the higher."[10]

As a motto to *The Interpretation of Dreams,* Freud quotes from the *Aeneid:* "Flectere si nequeo superos, Acheronta movebo" ["If I am unable to bend the gods above, I shall move the Underworld"]. Neo-platonic "topocosmos" reappear in Freud's "superego" and the under-world: the repressed, the unconscious, the id. In *Three Contributions to the Theory of Sex* Freud wrote: "The omnipotence of sex nowhere perhaps shows itself stronger than in this one of her aberrations. The highest and lowest in sexuality are everywhere most intimately con-nected ('From heaven through the world to hell')."[11]

In the Neoplatonic exchange of signs on the vertical axis, the celestial Venus is situated above, the Venus of animal sex below, the sphere of the intellect. As in a mountain lake whose depths reflect the peaks of nearby mountains, the signs of the "bottom" are the image and the repetition of the "top." *Venus vulgaris,* blind pleasure of sex, animal desire, *Amor ferinus,* becomes "a tool of the divine," as Ficino called it, an initiation into mysteries which, as in Paul, "eye hath not seen, nor ear heard." "Love is said by Orpheus," wrote Mirandola, "to be with-out eyes, because he is above the intellect." Above and at the same time below. For the Neoplatonists the descent to the bottom is also an ascent into heaven. Darkness is only *another* lighting. Blindness is only *another* seeing.[12] Quoting Homer, Tiresias, and Paul as examples, Mirandola wrote: "many who were rapt to the vision of spiritual beauty were by the same cause blinded in their corporeal eyes."[13] To the cave prisoners of Plato's parable everything seen is but a shadow. Shadows are nothing but imperfect reflections of true beings and things outside the cave. But the shadow indicates the source of the light. "Shadow," a word frequently used by Shakespeare, has many meanings, including "double" and "actor." Oberon, in *A Midsummer Night's Dream,* is called the "king of shadows," and Theseus says of theater: "The best in this kind are but shadows" (V.i.210). Theater is a shadow, that is, a double. "Revelry" means also "revelation." In the Neoplatonic code the "revels" and plays performed by the actor-shadows are, like dreams, texts with a latent content. According to Ficino:

And it may be said that the mind has two powers. . . . The one is the vision of the sober mind, the other is the mind in a state of love: for when it loses its reason by becoming drunk with nectar, then it enters into a state of love, diffusing itself wholly into delight: and it is better for it thus to rage than to remain aloof from that drunkenness.

This paraphrased translation from the *Enneads* of Plotinus could also be read as a Neoplatonic interpretation of Apuleius' *Metamorphoses.* In his famous commentary on the second Renaissance edition of *The Golden Ass* in 1600, Beroaldus quotes amply from Plato, Proclus, and Origen and sees in Apuleius' *Metamorphoses* the covert story and the mystical initiation into the mysteries of divine love: "For Plato writes in the *Symposium* that the eyes of the mind begin to see clearly when the eyes of the body begin to fail."[14]

This commentary might surprise a reader not familiar with the Neoplatonic exchange of signs, who reads in a straightforward way the crude story of Lucius transformed into an ass. His mistress, a maid in a witch's house, confused magic ointments and transformed him into a quadruped instead of a bird. Beaten, kicked, and starved by his successive owners, he wanders in his new shape through Thessaly all the way to Corinth. He witnesses kidnappings, murders, and rapes; sits with bandits in their cave; attends the blasphemous rituals of sodomites and eunuch priests; and nearly dies of exhaustion harnessed with slaves in a mill-house.

The *Satyricon* and *The Golden Ass,* like the picaresque novella later, use the device of fictional autobiography; these plots have an episodic construction. Each of the successive episodes yields a dry, realistic picture of human cruelty, of lust for power, and untamed sex. Transformed into a thinking animal, Lucius wanders among unthinking men-animals. The most drastic and shocking episode is the meeting between Lucius, who performs tricks as a trained donkey in the circus, and the new Pasiphae, a wealthy Corinthian matron who, like Titania sprayed with love potion, has a specific urge for asses: "Thou art he whom I love, thou art he whom I onely desire."

The infatuation of lunar Titania with a "sweet bully Bottom" ("So is mine eye enthralled to thy shape"[III.i.134]) is written under the spell of Apuleius: "how I should with my huge and great legs embrace so faire a Matron, or how I should touch her fine, dainty and silke skinne, with my hard hoofes, or how it was possible to kisse her soft, her pretty and ruddy lips, with my monstrous great mouth and stony teeth, or how she, who was so young and tender, could be able to receive me."[15]

Lucius is fearful that his monstrous endowment might "hurt the woman by any kind of meane," but the Greek Titania hastens to dispel his fears: "I hold thee my cunny, I hold thee my nops, my sparrow, and therewithal she eftsoones embraced my body round about." Even the grotesque humor of this sexual scene was repeated in *A Midsummer Night's Dream:*

> Come, sit thee down upon this flowery bed,
> While, I thy amiable cheeks do coy,
> And stick musk-roses in thy sleek smooth head,
> And kiss thy fair large ears, my gentle joy.

> (IV.i.1–4)

But *The Golden Ass* contains yet another story inserted into the realistic train of Lucius' adventures in the ass's shape. The love story of Cupid and Psyche, an *"anilibus fabula,"* "a pleasant old wives' tale," as Adlington calls it, may be the oldest literary version of the fable of "Beauty and the Beast."[16] The fable is known in folk traditions of many nations and distant cultures: catalogues of folk motifs place it in Scandinavia and Sicily, in Portugal and Russia. It also appears in India. In all versions of the fable, a young maiden who is to marry a prince is forbidden to look at her husband at night. At daytime he is a beautiful youth; at night she is happy with him. But she never sees him at night and is anxious to know with whom she is sleeping. When she lights the lamp in the bedroom, the lover turns out to be an animal: a white wolf, a bear, an ass in one Hindu version, and most often a monstrous snake. When the wife breaks the night–rule, the husband/night animal departs or dies. In *The Golden Ass* this tale is told in the bandits' cave by "the trifling and drunken old woman" to a virgin named Charite, abducted on the eve of her wedding and threatened with being sold to a brothel. This shocking, realistic frame for the mythical tale of Cupid and Psyche contributes its own significance to the opposition of the "top" and the "bottom" in Apuleius.

Venus herself was jealous of the princess Psyche, the most beautiful of all mortals. She sent out her own son, winged Cupid, to humiliate

Psyche and to hit the beauty with one of his "piercing darts" to make her fall madly in love "with the most miserablest creature living, the most poore, the most crooked and the most vile, that there may be none found in all the world of like wretchedness." Afterward, like Shakespeare's Titania, she would "wake when some vile thing is near" (II.ii.33). But Cupid fell in love with Psyche and married her under the condition that she would never cast her eyes upon him in bed. Psyche broke her vow and lit a lamp. A drop of hot oil sputtered from the lamp and Cupid, burnt, ran off forever.

The story of Psyche ends with her giving birth to a daughter called Voluptas. The story of Lucius' transformation ends with his resumption of human form and his initiation first into the mysteries of Isis and, after the return to Rome, into the rites of Osiris. Initiations are costly, but Lucius, a lawyer in the *collegium* established by Sulla, is able to pay the price of secret rites. The story of Psyche, the most beautiful of all mortal maidens, leads from beauty through the tortures of love to eternal pleasure. The story of Lucius, always sexually fascinated by hair before his own transformation into a hairy ass, leads from earthy delights to humiliating baldness: he was ordered twice to shave his head as a high priest of Isis and Osiris.

For Bakhtin, the tradition of *serio ludere* starts with the Menippean satire, Petronius and Apuleius. But which of the two metamorphoses in *The Golden Ass* is *serio,* and in which does one hear only the mocking *risus?*

For Beroaldus, *Metamorphoses* is a Platonic message of transcendent love, written in a cryptic language on two levels above and below reason. From Boccaccio's *Genealogia Deorum* (1472) to Calderon's *auto sacramental,* where the story of Psyche and Amor symbolizes the mystical marriage of the Church and Christ and ends with the glorification of the Eucharist, Apuleius was often read as an orphic, Platonic, or Christian allegory of mystical rapture or divine fury.

But for at least three centuries *The Golden Ass* was also read in the code of "serious laughter." In *Decameron,* two novellae were adopted from Apuleius. In *Don Quixote,* the episode of the charge on the jugs of wine was repeated after *Metamorphoses.* Adaptations are innumerable: from Moliere's *Psyche,* La Fontaine's *Les Amours du Psyche et Cupide,* Le Sage's *Gil Blas,* to Anatole France's *La Rotisserie de la Reine Pedauque.*[17]

In both the intellectual traditions and the codes of interpretation there are exchanges of icons and signs between the "top" and "bottom," the above and below reason. In the "Platonic translation," where the "above" *logos* outside the cave is the sole truth and the "below" is merely its murky shadow, the signs of the "top" are the ultimate verification of the signs of the bottom. *Venus vulgaris* is but a reflection and a presentment of the Celestial Venus. In *serio ludere* the "top" is only *mythos;* the bottom is the human condition. The signs and icons of the "bottom" are the ultimate test of the signs and icons of the "top." *Venus celestiae* is merely a projection, a mythical representation of *Amore bestiale*—sexual desire. The true Olympus is the Hades of Lucian's *Dialogues of the Dead* or of Aristophanes' *Frogs,* where the coward and buffoon Dionysus appears in the cloak of Hercules. Having its origins in Saturnalia, *serio ludere* is the sacred drolerie, a festive *parodia sacra.*

In hermetic interpretations, the *fabula* of Psyche and Cupid is a decoding of Lucius' metamorphosis. Transformation into a donkey is here a covert story whose mystical sense is concealed. Within the "carnival" as a code, Lucius' adventures in an ass's skin form an overt story uncovering the mockery in the tale of Amor and Cupid.

Psyche's two sisters, jealous of her excellent marriage, convinced her that she shared her bed with a snake and monster. Poor Psyche's mind was troubled since "at least *in one person* she hateth the beast *(bestiam)* and loveth her husband." As in dream symbolism, the latent content of the story of Psyche and Cupid becomes manifest in Lucius' adventures. The signs of the "top" are an inversion and a displacement of the signs of the "bottom." Like the Corinthian matron, fascinated by "monstrosity," and like Titania, aroused by Bottom's "beastliness," Psyche *loved* the beast and *hated* the husband "in one person." The evil sisters, like a Freudian analyst, uncovered her deep secret: "this servile and dangerous pleasure [clandestinae Veneris faetidi periculesique concubitus] . . . do more delight thee."

In both code systems, the Neoplatonic and the *serio ludere* of the carnival, the microcosm represents and repeats the macrocosm, and man is the image of the universe. In these models with their vertical imagery man is divided in half: from the waist up he represents the heavens, from the waist down, hell. But all hells, from the antique Tartarus through the hells of Dante and Bosch, are the image of Earth.

> Down from the waist they are Centaurs,
> Though woman all above:
> But to the girdle do the Gods inherit,
> Beneath is all the fiend's:
> There's hell, there's darkness.
>
> *(King Lear,* IV.vi.123–30)

In both systems the signs of the "above" and the "below," the *macro,* and the *micro,* correspond to each other and are exchangeable. But their values are opposed both in the Neoplatonic code and in the carnival tradition and, to a certain extent, in the poetics of tragedy and comedy. From the Saturnalia through the medieval and Renaissance carnivals and celebrations, the elevated and noble attributes of the human mind are exchanged—as Bakhtin shows convincingly—for the bodily functions (with a particular emphasis on the "lower stratum": digestion, defecation, urination, copulation, and labor). In carnival wisdom they are the essence of life: a guarantee of its continuity.

In Shakespeare's adoption of motifs from *The Golden Ass,* most significant is the concoction of Psyche and the Corinthian matron within the character of Titania. Titania was punished like Psyche. The punishment is infatuation with the most "base and vile" of human beings. But this vile and base person is not transformed Cupid but the Bacchic donkey. Titania sleeps with this carnival ass like the Corinthian matron of Apuleius' *Metamorphoses.* In the genre of *serio ludere* seriousness does not exist as separate from mockery. Seriousness is mockery and mockery is seriousness.

The exchange of signs in *serio ludere* is the very same translation into the bottom, the low, the base, and the obscene that takes place in folk rituals and carnival processions.[18] The masterpiece of carnivalesque literature is Rabelais's *Gargantua and Pantagruel.* In the sixth chapter of the first book of *Gargantua,* Gergamelle feels birth pangs:

> A few moments later, she began to groan, lament and cry out. Suddenly crowds of midwives came rushing in from all directions. Feeling and groping her below, they found certain loose shreds of skin, of a rather unsavory odor, which they took to be a child. It was, on the contrary, her fundament which had escaped with the mollification of her right intestine (you call it the bumgut) because she had eaten too much tripe.[19]

Gargantua's mother gorged herself so much the previous evening that the child found its natural exit blocked in this carnival physiology.

> As a result of Gargamelle's discomfort, the cotyledons of the placenta of her matrix were enlarged. The child, leaping through the breach and entering the hollow vein, ascended through her diaphragm to a point above her shoulders. Here the vein divides into two: the child accordingly worked his way in a sinistral direction, to issue, finally, through the left ear.

In medieval moral treatises and sermons, the mystery of the immaculate conception was explained again and again as the voice of the Holy Ghost entering the Virgin Mary through her ear—invariably, through her left ear. But there is more to this birth of Gargantua than *parodia sacra*, as is shown by Claude Gaignebet in his excellent work on *Le Carnaval*. The Holy Ghost descended to the Virgin Mary from the top to the bottom so she could conceive immaculately. A blow from the anus propelled Gargantua from the bottom to the top so the child of carnival could be born in the upside–down world.[20] In this bottom translation, earthly *pneuma* replaced the divine one and the movement along the vertical axis was reversed.

Significantly, St. Paul of the Corinthians is the patron of this carnival birth. Rabelais appeals directly to Corinthians:

Now I suspect that you do not thoroughly believe this strange nativity. If you do not, I care but little, though an honest and sensible man believes what he is told and what he finds written. Does not Solomon say in *Proverbs* (14:15): "*Innocens credit omni verbo,* the innocent believeth every word," and does not St. Paul (1 Corinthians 13) declare: "*Charitas omnia credit,*" Charity believeth all?[21]

In the early Renaissance, Paul became the patron saint of sacred *drolerie*. In the carnivalesque literature of *serio ludere,* the first letter to the Corinthians is quoted as often as in the writings of the Neoplatonists. And the choice of the most favored quotes is nearly the same:

Where *is* the wise? where *is* the scribe? where *is* the disputer of this world? hath not God made foolish the wisdom of the world? (1.20)

And base things of the world, and things which are despised, hath God chosen, *yea,* and things which are not, to bring to naught things that are. (1.28)

If any among you seemeth to be wise in this world, let him become a fool, that he may be wise. For the wisdom of this world is foolishness with God. (3.18–19)

For the Florentine Neoplatonists, Paul is the teacher of *supra intellectum* mysteries. But within the semiotics of the carnival, the fool is wise and folly is the wisdom of this world.[22] For Rabelais, and perhaps even more so for Erasmus, the letter to the Corinthians was the praise of folly:

"Therfore *Salomon* beyng so great a kynge, was naught ashamed of my name when he saied in his .XXX. chapitre, '*I am most foole of all men:*' Nor *Paule doctour of the gentiles* . . . when writing to the *Corinthians* he said: '*I speake it as vnvise, that I more than others, etc.,*' as who saieth it were a great dishonour for him to be ouercome in folie" (109.29f).

In Erasmus' *Moriae enconium* Folly speaks in first person and in its own name. In this most Menippean of Renaissance treatises, Folly appeals to Paul's "foolishness of God" on nearly every page. Near the end of *The Praise of Folly,* Erasmus describes heavenly raptures which rarely occurring to mortals, may give the foretaste or "savour of that hieghest rewarde" and which, as in Pau1, "was neuer mans eie sawe, nor eare heard." But Erasmus' Folly, ever cynical and joyful, is more interested in returning to earth and awakening than in mystical raptures.

> Who so euer therefore haue suche grace . . . by theyr life tyme to tast of this saied felicitee, they are subjecte to a certaine passion muche lyke vnto madnesse . . . or beyng in a traunce, thei doo speake certaine thynges not hangyng one with an other . . . and sodeinely without any apparent cause why, dooe chaunge the state of theyr countenaunces. For now shall ye see theim of glad chere, now of as sadde againe, now thei wepe, now thei laugh, now thei sighe, for briefe, it is certaine that they are wholly distraught and rapte out of theim selues. (128.4ff)

Bottom speaks much as Folly after awakening from his own dream:

> Man is but an ass, if he go about to expound his dream. Me-thought I was—there is no man can tell what. Methought I was—and methought I had—but man is but a patched fool if he will offer to say what methought I had. (IV.i.205–09)

We may now return to Erasmus:

> In sort, that whan a little after thei come againe to their former wittes, thei denie plainly thei wote where thei became, or whether thei were than in theyr bodies, or out of theyr bodies, wakyng or slepyng: remembring also as little, either what they heard, saw, saied, or did than, sauyng as it were through a cloude, or by a dreame: but this they know certainely, that whiles their mindes so roued and wandred, thei were most happie and blisfull, so that

they lament and wepe at theyr retourne vnto theyr former senses.
(128.16ff)

Let us now hear once more Bottom speaking to his fellows:

> *Bottom:* Masters, I am to discourse wonders: but ask me not what;
> for if I tell you, I am not a true Athenian. I will tell you every
> thing, right as it fell out.
> *Quince:* Let us hear, sweet Bottom.
> *Bottom:* Not a word of me. (IV.ii.27-32)

The Praise of Folly, dedicated to Thomas More, was published in
London in Chaloner's translation in 1549 and reprinted twice (1560,
1577) — the last time almost twenty years before *A Midsummer Night's
Dream.* It is hard to conceive that Shakespeare had never read one of
the most provocative books of the century.[23] Bottom's misquote from
Corinthians appears in the comical context of a sudden awakening after
the stay in "heaven." But this Bottom "heaven" is the asinine metamorphosis taken from Apuleius. Apuleius, Paul, and Erasmus meet in
Bottom's monologue. Of all encounters in *A Midsummer Night's Dream,*
this one is least expected. "I have had a most rare vision. I have had a
dream." The same word "vision(s)" was already uttered by Titania in a
preceding scene, upon her waking from a "dream": "My Oberon, what
visions have I seen! / Methought I was enamour'd of an ass"
(IV.i.75-76).

III

From Saturnalia to medieval *ludi* the ass is one of the main actors in
processions, comic rituals, and holiday revels. In Bakhtin's succinct
formula the ass is "the Gospel-symbol of debasement and humility (as
well as concommitant regeneration)." On festive days such as the
Twelfth Night, Plough Monday, the Feast of Fools, and the Feast of the
Ass, merry and often vulgar parodies of liturgy were allowed. On those
days devoted to general folly, clerics often participated as masters of
ceremony, and an "Asinine Mass" was the main event. An ass was
occasionally brought to the church, in which a hymn especially composed for the occasion would be sung:

> Orientis partibus
> Adventavit Asinus

Pulcher et fortissimus
Sarcinis aptissimus.

"Ass masses" were unknown in England, but the symbolism of the
carnival ass and sacred *drolerie* survived from the Middle Ages until
Elizabethan times.[24] At the beginning of Elizabeth's reign donkeys
dressed up as bishops or dogs with Hosts in their teeth would appear in
court masques. But more significant than these animal disguises, which
were a mockery of Catholic liturgy, was the appearance of the Bacchic
donkey on stage. In Nashe's *Summer's Last Will and Testament,* performed in Croyden in 1592 or 1593, a few years before *A Midsummer
Night's Dream,* Bacchus rode onto the stage atop an ass adorned with ivy
and garlands of grapes.

Among all festival masques of animals the figure of the ass is most
polysemic. The icon of an ass, for Bakhtin "the most ancient and lasting
symbol of the material bodily lower stratum," is the ritualistic and
carnivalesque mediator between heaven and earth, which transforms
the signs of the "top" into the signs of the "bottom." In its symbolic
function of translation from the high to the low, the ass appears both in
ancient tradition, in Apuleius, and in the Old and New Testament, as
Balaam's she-ass who spoke in a human voice to give testimony to
truth, and as the ass on which Jesus rode into Jerusalem for the last
time. "Tell ye the daughter of Si-on, Behold thy King cometh unto
thee, meek, and sitting upon an ass, and a colt foal of an ass" (Matt.
21.5).

The bodily meets with the spiritual in the *figura* and the masque of
the ass. Therefore, the mating of Bottom and the Queen of the Fairies,
which culminates the night and forest revelry, is so ambiguous and rich
in meanings. In traditional interpretations of *A Midsummer Night's
Dream,* the personae of the comedy belong to three different "worlds":
the court of Theseus and Hippolyta; the "Athenian" mechanicals; and
the "supernatural" world of Oberon, Titania, and the "fairies." But
particularly in this traditional interpretation, the night Titania spent
with an ass in her "consecrated bower" must appear all the stranger and
more unexpected.

Titania is the night double of Hippolyta, her dramatic and theatrical
paradigm. Perhaps, since during the Elizabethan period the doubling of
roles was very common, these two parts were performed by the same
young boy. This Elizabethan convention was taken up by Peter Brook in
his famous performance. But even if performed by different actors,
Hippolyta's metamorphosis into Titania and her return to the previous
state, like Theseus' transformation into Oberon, must have seemed

much more obvious and natural to Elizabethan patrons than to audiences brought up on conventions of nineteenth- and twentieth-century theater. *A Midsummer Night's Dream* was most likely performed at an aristocratic wedding where court spectators knew the icons as well as the rules of a masque.

Court masques during the early Tudor and Elizabethan period were composed of three sequels: (1) appearance in mythological or shepherds' costumes; (2) dancing, occasionally with recitation or song; and (3) the ending of the masque, during which the masquers invited the court audience to participate in a general dance. Professional actors did not take part in masques, which were courtly masquerades and social games. "Going off" or "taking out," as this last dance was called, constituted the end of metamorphosis and a return of the masquers to their proper places and distinctions at court.

The disguises in the masque corresponded to social distinctions. The hierarchies were preserved. Dukes and lords would never consent to represent anyone below the mythological standing of Theseus. Theseus himself could only assume the shape of the "King of the Fairies" and Hippolyta, the "Queen of the Fairies." The annual Records at the Office of the Revels document the figures that appeared in court masques. Among fifteen sets of masking garments in 1555, there were "Venetian senators," "Venuses," "Huntresses," and "Nymphs." During the Jacobean period Nymphs of English rivers were added to the Amazons and Nymphs accompanying Diana, and Oberon with his knights was added to Acteon and his hunters. In 1611, nearly fifteen years after *A Midsummer Night's Dream,* young Henry, the king's son, appeared in the costume of the "faery Prince" in Jonson's *Oberon.*[25]

The most frequent and popular figure of both courtly and wedding masque was Cupid. On a painting representing the wedding masque of Henry Unton in 1572, the guests seated at a table watch a procession of ten Cupids (five white ones and five black ones) accompanied by Mercury, Diana, and her six nymphs.[26]

From the early Tudor masque to the sophisticated spectacles at the court of Inigo Jones, Cupid appears with golden wings, in the same attire, and with the same accessories: "a small boye to be cladd in a canvas hose and doblett sylverd over with a payre of winges of gold with bow and aroves, his eyes bended."[27] This Cupid—with or without a blindfold—would randomly shoot his arrows at shepherdesses, sometimes missing:

> But I might see young Cupid's fiery shaft
> Quenched in the chaste beams of the watery moon;

And the imperial votress passed on.

(II.i.161–63)

But the Renaissance Cupid, who appears eight times in the poetic discourse of *A Midsummer Night's Dream,* has a different name, a different costume, and a different language as a person on stage. The blindfolded Cupid is "Anglicised" or "translated" into Puck, or Robin Goodfellow. On the oldest woodcut representing the folk Robin Goodfellow, in the 1628 story of his "Mad Pranks and Merry Jests," he holds in his right hand a large phallic candle and in his left hand a large broom. He has goat's horns on his head and goat's cloven feet. He is wearing only a skirt made of animal skins and is accompanied by black figures of men and women dressed in contemporary English garments and dancing in a circle. This "folk" Robin Goodfellow is still half a Satyr or Pan dancing with Nymphs.

The oldest image of Robin Goodfellow might refresh the imagination of scenographers and directors of *A Midsummer Night's Dream* who still see Puck as Romantic elf. But this engraving appears significant also for the interpretation of *A Midsummer Night's Dream,* where Shakespeare's wonderful syncretism mixes mythological icons of court masques with folk carnival. In *A Midsummer Night's Dream* mythological arrows are replaced by the folk love potion. In the poetic discourse this love potion still comes from the flower which turns red from Cupid's shaft. Shakespeare might have found the "love juice" in Montemayer's pastoral *Diana,* but he transposed the conventional simile into a sharp and brutal visual sign, the stage metaphor in which Puck sprays love juice in the eyes of the sleeping lovers.

"And maidens call it 'love-in-idleness'" (II.i.168). The flower's real name is pansy. Its other folk names are "Fancy," "Kiss me," "Cull me" or "Cuddle me to you," "Tickle my fancy," "Kiss me ere I arise," "Kiss me at the garden gate," and "Pink of my John."[28] These are "bottom translations" of Cupid's shaft.

But in the discourse of *A Midsummer Night's Dream* there is not one flower, but two: "love-in- idleness" and its antidote. The opposition of "blind Cupid" and of Cupid with an "incorporeal eye" is translated into the opposition of mythic flowers: "Diana's bud e'er Cupid's flower / Hath ever such force and blessed power" (IV.i.72–73).

The Neoplatonic unity of Love and Chastity is personified in the transformation of Venus into virginal Diana. Neoplatonists borrowed this exchange of signs from a line in Vergil's *Aeneid,* in which Venus appears to Aeneas as *virginis arma:* "on her shoulder she carried a bow as a huntress would" (i.327). In the semantics of emblems, the bow, weapon of Cupid-love, and the bow, weapon of Amazon-virgo, was a mediation between Venus and Diana. The harmony of the bow, as Plato called it, was for Pico "harmony in discord," a unity of opposites.[29] From the union of Cupid and Psyche, brutally interrupted on Earth, the daughter Voluptas was born in the heavens; from the adulterous relation of Mars and Venus, the daughter Harmony was born. Harmony, as Neoplatonists repeated after Ovid, Horace, and Plutarch, is *concordia discors* and *discordia concors*.

For Elizabethan poets and for carpenters who prepared court masques and entertainments, the exchange of icons and emblems became unexpectedly useful in the cult of the Virgin Queen. The transformation of Venus into Diana allowed them to praise Elizabeth simultaneously under the names of Cynthia/Diana and Venus, the goddess of love. In Paris's judgment, as Giordano Bruno explicated in *Eroici furori,* the apple awarded to the most beautiful goddess was symbolically given to the other two goddesses as well: "for in the simplicity of divine essence . . . all these perfections are equal because they are infinite."[30]

George Peele must have read Bruno. In his *Arraignement of Paris,* the first extant English pastoral play with songs and dances by nymphs and shepherdesses, Paris hands the golden ball to Venus.[31] When offended, Diana appeals to the gods on Olympus; the golden orb is finally delivered to Elizabeth, "queen of Second Troy." The nymph Elise is "Queen Juno's peer" and "Minerva's mate": "As fair and lovely as the Queen of Love / As chaste as Dian in her chaste desires" (V.i.86–87).

In Ovid's *Metamorphoses,* "Titania" is one of Diana's names. Titania, in *A Midsummer Night's Dream,* appears without a bow. The bow is an emblem of the Queen of Amazons. In the first scene of act I, Hippolyta in her first lines evokes the image of a bow: "And then the moon, like to a silver bow /Now-bent in heaven, shall behold the night / Of our solemnities" (I.i.9-11). Liturgical carnival starts with the new moon after the winter solstice. The new moon, like the letter *D,* resembles a strung bow. The moon, the "governess of floods" (II.i.103), is a sign of Titania; her nocturnal sports are "moonlight revels" (II.i.141). In the poetical discourse the bow of the Amazons and the bow of the moon relate Hippolyta and Titania.

A sophisticated game of the court, with allegorical eulogies and allusions, is played through the exchange of classical emblems later called "hieroglyphiches" by Ben Jonson. Greek Arcadia was slowly moving from Italy to England. Mythical figures and classical themes in masques, entertainments, and plays easily lent themselves to pastoral settings. But in this new pastoral mode the "Queen of the fairies" was still an allegory of Elizabeth. For the Entertainment of Elvetham behind the palace at the base of wooded hills, an artificial pond in the shape of a half-moon had been constructed. On an islet in the middle, the fairies dance with their queen, singing a song to the music of a consort:

> *Elisa* is the fairest Queene
> That euer trod vpon this greene . . .
> O blessed bee each day and houre,
> Where sweete *Elisa* builds her bowre.

The queen of the fairies, with a garland as an imperial crown, recites in blank verse:

> I that abide in places under-ground
> Aureola, the Queene of Fairy Land
> . . . salute you with this chaplet,
> Giuen me by Auberon, the fairy King.

The Entertainment at Elvetham took place in the autumn of 1591, only a few years before even the latest possible date of *A Midsummer Night's Dream*. Even if Shakespeare had not attended it, this magnificent event was prepared by poets, artists, and musicians with whom he was acquainted. The quarto with the libretto, the lyrics, and the songs of the four-day spectacle in Elizabeth's honor, was published and twice reprinted.[32] Oberon, Titania, and the fairies did not enter the Shakespearean comedy from old romances such as *Huon of Bordeaux,* but from the stage: perhaps from Greene's play *James IV* in which Oberon dances with the fairies and most certainly from Elizabethan masque and entertainment.

In masques and court pastorals, among the mythological figures next to Cupid we always find Mercury. In *A Midsummer Night's Dream* it appears that the place usually assigned to Mercury is empty. But Mercury is not merely the messenger, the *psychopompos* who induces and interrupts sleep as Puck and Ariel do.[33] Hermes-Mercury belongs to the family of tricksters. The trickster is the most invariable, universal, and constant mythic character in the folklore of all peoples. As a mediator between gods and men—the bottom and the top—the trickster is a special broker: he both deceives the gods and cheats men. The trickster is the personification of mobility and changeability and transcends all boundaries, overthrowing all hierarchies. He turns everything upside-down. Within this world gone mad a new order emerges from chaos, and life's continuity is renewed.[34]

> Jack shall have Jill,
> Nought shall go ill;
> The man shall have his mare again, and all shall be well.
>
> (III.ii.461-63)

In the marvelous syncretism of *A Midsummer Night's Dream,* Puck the trickster is a bottom and carnivalesque translation of Cupid, Mercury, and Satyr.[35] The Harlequin, Fool, and Lord of Misrule—called in Scotland the Abbot of Unreason—belong to this theatrical family of Tricksters. Puck's practical joke ("An ass's noll I fixed on his head" [III.ii.17]) has its origin in the oldest tradition of folk festivities. Mummery, painting the face red or white, or putting grotesque or animal masques on the face, is still often seen during Twelfth Night, Ash Wednesday, or Valentine's Day.

But putting on an ass's head was not only a theatrical repetition of mockeries and jokes of the Feast of Fools or the day of Boy-Bishop. Another universal rite is also repeated when a "boore," a thing "base and vile," or a mock-king of the carnival was crowned, and after his short reign, uncrowned, thrashed, mocked, and abused. As the drunk Christopher Sly, a tinker, is led into the palace in *The Taming of the Shrew,* so the bully Bottom is introduced to Titania's court of fairies. A coronet of flowers winds through his hairy temples as a crown and the queen's servants fulfill all his fancies. Among Bottom's colleagues is also another "Athenian" tinker, Tom Snout. Like Christopher Sly and all mock-kings abused and uncrowned, Bottom wakes from his dream having played only the part of an ass.

The painting by Henry Fuseli, who was one of the most original illustrators of Shakespeare's plays, depicts Titania assuming the pose of Leonardo's *Leda.* She is nude, but her hair is carefully coiffed. She is calling upon her servants, but her eyes are half-closed as if in ecstasy. Next to Titania sits Bottom, hunched over. He appears sad or surprised. He is paying no attention to Titania or to Peaseblossom who is scratching his head. Titania's court—dwarfs, midgets, and ladies in waiting—is wearing Empire dresses. Bottom with his ass's head found himself at some court masque or feast whose sense he does not seem to grasp. Fuseli's painting dates from ca.1780-1790.

Both in traditional performances of *A Midsummer Night's Dream,* in which Bottom's night at Titania's court is presented as a romantic ballet, and in the spectacle by Peter Brook and many of his followers emphasizing Titania's sexual fascination with a monstrous phallus (mea culpa!), the carnival ritual of Bottom's adventure was altogether lost. Even Lucius, as a frustrated ass in Apuleius, was amazed at the sexual eagerness of the Corinthian matron who, having "put off all her garments to her naked skinne . . . began to annoint all her body with balme" and caressed him more adeptly than "in the Courtsan schooles." Bottom appreciates being treated as a very important person, but is more interested in food than in the bodily charms of Titania.

In Bottom's metamorphosis and in his encounters with Titania, not only do high and low, metaphysics and physics, and poetry and farce meet, but so do two theatrical traditions: the masque and the court entertainment meet the carnival world turned upside-down.[36] In masques and entertainments, "noble" characters were sometimes accompanied by Barbarians, Wild Men, Fishwives, and Marketwives. At the Entertainment at Elvetham an "ugly" Nereus showed up, frightening the court ladies.[37] But for the first time in both the history of revels and the history of theater, Titania/Diana/the Queen of Fairies sleeps with a donkey in her "flowery bower."[38] This encounter of Titania and Bottom, the ass and the mock-king of the carnival, is the very beginning of modern comedy and one of its glorious opening nights.

IV

A musical interlude accompanies the transition from night to day in *A Midsummer Night's Dream:* "Winde Hornes, Enter Theseus, Egeus, Hippolita, and all his traine" (Stage Direction IV.i.101 *Folio).* In this poetic discourse, the blowing of the hunters' horns, the barking of the hounds, and the echo from the mountains are translated into a musical opposition in the Platonic tradition of "discord" and "concord." In this opposition between day and night, not the night but precisely the musical orchestration of daybreak is called discord by Theseus and by Hippolyta. For Theseus this discord marks "the musical confusion / Of hounds and echo in conjunction" (IV.i.109-10). "I never heard," replies Hippolyta, "so musical a discord, such sweet thunder" (116-17). Only a few lines further, when Lysander and Demetrius kneel at Theseus' feet after the end of "night-rule," the "discord" of the night turns into the new "concord" of the day: "I know you two are rival enemies. / How comes this gentle concord in the world" (IV.i.142).[39]

Both terms of the opposition, "concord" and "discord," are connected by Theseus when Philostrate, his master of the revels, hands him the brief of an interlude to be presented by the "Athenian" mechanicals:

> 'A tedious brief scene of young Pyramus
> And his love Thisbe; very tragical mirth.'?
> Merry and tragical? Tedious and brief?
> That is hot ice and wondrous strange snow!
> How shall we find the concord of this discord?
>
> (V.i.56–60)

This new *concordia discors* is a tragicomedy, and good Peter Quince gives a perfect definition of it when he tells the title of the play to his actors: "Marry, our play is 'The most lamentable comedy, and most cruel death of Pyramus and Thisbe'" (I.ii.11–12). Although merely an Athenian carpenter, as it turns out, Quince is quite well-read in English repertory, having styled the title of his play after the "new tragical comedy" *Damon and Pithias* by Edwards (1565), or after Preston's *Cambises* (published ca. 1570), a "lamentable comedy mixed full of pleasant mirth."[40] The same traditional titles, judged by printers to be attractive to readers and spectators, appeared on playbills and title pages of quartos: *The comicall History of the Merchant of Venice* or *The most Excellent and lamentable Tragedie of Romeo and Iuliet.* This last title would fit better the story of Pyramus and Thisbe.

We do not know and probably will not discover which of the plays, *Romeo and Juliet* or *A Midsummer Night's Dream,* was written earlier. History repeats itself twice, "the first time as tragedy, the second as farce." Marx was right: world history and the theater teach us that *opera buffa* repeats the protagonists and situations of *opera seria.* The "most cruel death" of Romeo and Juliet is changed into a comedy, but this comedy is "lamentable." The new tragicomedy, "concord of the discord," is a *double* translation of tragedy into a comedy and of comedy into burlesquing. The burlesque and the parody are not only in the dialogue and in the songs; the "lamentable comedy" is played at Theseus' wedding by the clowns.

Burlesque is first the acting and stage business. A wall separates the lovers, and they can only whisper and try to kiss through a "hole," a "cranny," or "chink." This scene's crudity is both naive and sordid, as in sophomoric jokes and jests where obscene senses are given to innocent words. Gestures here are more lewd than words.

The Wall was played by Snout. Bottom, who also meddled in directing, recommended: "Let him hold his fingers thus" (III.i.65–66). But what was this gesture supposed to be? Neither the text nor stage directions ("Wall stretches out his fingers" [Stage Direction V.i.175]) are clear. In the nineteenth–century tradition, the Wall stretched out his fingers while the lovers kissed through the "cranny." In Peter Hall's Royal Shakespeare Company film (1969), the Wall holds in his hands a brick which he puts between his legs. Only then does he make a "cranny" with his thumb and index finger. But it could have been yet another gesture. The "hole," as the letter V made by the middle and index finger, would be horizontal and vertical. As Thomas Clayton argues, Snout in the Elizabethan theater of clowns straddled and stretched out his fingers between his legs wide apart. "And this the cranny is, right and sinister" (V.i.162). Snout, although an "Athenian" tinker, had a taste of Latin or Italian and knew what "sinister" meant.[41]

Romeo could not even touch Juliet when she leaned out the window. The Wall scene ("O kiss me through the hole of this vile wall" [198]) is the "bottom translation" of the balcony scene from *Romeo and Juliet*. The sequel of suicides is the same in both plays. But Thisby "dies" differently. The burlesque Juliet on stage stabs herself perforce with the scabbard of Pyramus' sword.[42] This is all we know for certain about how *A Midsummer Night's Dream* was performed in Shakespeare's lifetime.

The lovers from Athens did not meet a lion during their nightly adventure as Pyramus and Thisbe did in their forest, nor a dangerous lioness as Oliver and Orlando did in the very similar Arden forest of *As You Like It*. But the menace of death hovers over the couple from the very beginning: "Either to die the death, or to abjure" (I.i.65). The *furor* of love always calls forth death as its only equal partner. Hermia says to Lysander: "Either death or you I'll find immediately" (II.ii.155); Lysander says of Helena: "Whom I do love, and will do till my death" (III.ii.167); Helena says of Demetrius: "To die upon the hand I love so well" (II.i.244), and again: " 'tis partly my own fault, / Which death, or absence soon shall remedy" (III.ii.243–44). Even sleep "with leaden legs and batty wings" is "death counterfeiting" (III.ii.364).

In these four voices of love frenzy, neither the classical Cupid with his "fiery shaft" nor the Neoplatonic Cupid with his "incorporeal eye" are present any longer. Desire ceases to use a paradigmatic language. Now desire is the action of the body: the hand which grabs for another hand to throw someone to the ground or to kill. The words "death" and "dead" are uttered twenty–eight times; "dying" and "die" occur fourteen times. Altogether, the linguistic field of "death" appears in nearly fifty verses of *A Midsummer Night's Dream* and is distributed almost evenly among the events in the forest and the play at Theseus' wedding.

The frequency of "kill" and "killing" is thirteen, and "sick" and "sickness" occur six times. In *A Midsummer Night's Dream,* which has often been called a happy comedy of love, "kiss" and "kissing" occur only six times, always within the context of the burlesque; "joy" occurs eight times, "happy" six, and "happiness" none.

The forest happenings during the premarital night are only the first revels and sports in *A Midsummer Night's Dream;* the main merriment is provided by clowns. In the "mirths," in the forest and at court, Bottom is the leading actor. While rehearsing his part in the forest, "sweet Pyramus" was "translated" into an ass. He "dies" on stage as Pyramus, only to be called an ass by Theseus: "With the help of a surgeon, he might yet recover, and prove an ass" (V.i.298–300).

If Bottom's metamorphoses in the forest and at court are read synchronically, as one reads a musical score, the "sweet bully" boy in both of his roles—as an ass and as Pyramus—sleeps with the queen of the fairies, is crowned and uncrowned, dies, and is resurrected on stage. The true director of the night–rule in the woods is Puck, the Lord of Misrule. The interlude of Pyramus and Thisbe was chosen for the wedding ceremonies by Philostrate, the master of revels to Theseus. Within *A Midsummer Night's Dream,* performed as an interlude at an aristocratic wedding, the play within a play is a paradigm of comedy as a whole. *A Midsummer Night's Dream* has an enveloping structure: the small "box" repeats the larger one, as a Russian doll contains smaller ones.

The brutal and violent change of desire during a single night and the pre–wedding night with a "monster" do not appear to be the most appropriate themes for wedding entertainment. Neither is the burlesque suicide of the antique models of Romeo and Juliet the most appropriate merriment for "a feast in great solemnity."[43] All dignity and seriousness is absent from the presentation of "most cruel death of Pyramus and Thisbe." The night adventures of Titania and two young couples is finally nullified and reduced to a "dream."

"The lunatic, the lover and the poet, / Are of imagination all compact" (V.i.7–8). These lines of Theseus, like those of Helena's monologue from the first scene in act I, are a part of the poetic metadiscourse whose theme is self- referent: the dreams in *A Midsummer Night's Dream* and the whole play. And as in Helena's soliloquy, Neoplatonic oppositions return in it.

Ficino, in *In Platonis Phaedrum* and in *De amore,* distinguishes four forms of inspired madness—*furor divinus:* the "fine frenzy" of the poet; "the ravishment of the diviner"; "the prophetic rapture of the mystic"; and the "ecstasy of the lover"—*furor amatorius.*[44]

Even more important than the repetition of Neoplatonic categories of "madness" is the inversion by Theseus/Shakespeare of the values and hierarchy in this exchange of signs:

> The poet's eye, in a fine frenzy rolling,
> Doth glance from heaven to earth, from earth to heaven;
> And as imagination bodies forth
> The forms of things unknown, the poet's pen
> Turns them to shapes, and gives to airy nothing
> A local habitation and a name.
>
> (V.i.12–17)

As opposed to the "fine frenzy" of the Platonic poet, Shakespeare's pen gives earthly names to shadows, "airy nothing," and relocates them on earth.[45] The "lunatic" who "sees more devil than vast hell can hold" (V.i.9) replaces Neoplatonic mystics. The frenzied lover "sees Helen's beauty in a brow of Egypt" (V.i.11). All three—"the lunatic, the lover, and the poet"—are similar to a Don Quixote who also gave in to phantasies, shadows of wandering knights, the "local habitation and a name"; who saw beautiful Dulcinea in an ugly country maid; and, like a Shakespearean madman who in a "bush supposed a bear" (V.i.22) would charge windmills with his lance, taking them to be wizards, and stormed wineskins, thinking them to be brigands.

> Lovers and madmen have such seething brigands,
> Such shaping phantasies, that apprehend
> More than cool reason ever comprehends.
>
> (V.i.4–6)

In this metadiscourse, which is at the same time self–defeating and self–defending, a manifesto of Shakespeare's dramatic art and a defense of his comedy are contained. "More than cool reason ever comprehends" is not the Platonic "shadow" and the metaphysical *supra intellectum* of Pico and Ficino. "More than cool reason ever comprehends" is, as in Paul, the "foolish things of the world" which God designed "to confound the wise." This "foolishness of God," taken from the Corinthians, read and repeated after the carnival tradition, is the defense of the Fool and the praise of Folly.

The lunatics—the Fool, the Lord of Misrule, the Abbott of Unreason—know well that when a true king, as well as the carnival mock-king, is thrown off, he is turned into a thing "base and vile, holding no quantity"; that on Earth there are "more devils than vast hell can hold" and that Dianas, Psyches, and Titanias sleep not with winged Cupids but with asses; but what is this Bacchic ass of Saturnalia and carnival? "Bless thee, Bottom, bless the! Thou are translated" (III.i.113). The Bottom translation is the wisdom and the language of the Fool.

V

Bottom, soon after his theatrical death on stage, springs up and bids farewell to Wall with an indecent gesture. Thisbe is also resurrected; her body cannot remain on stage. The merry, joyful, and playful Bergomask ends the clowns' spectacle. It is midnight and all three pairs of lovers are anxious to go to bed. In a ceremonious procession they leave the stage, illuminated by the torchbearers.

The stage is now empty for a moment. If *A Midsummer Night's Dream* was performed in the evening during the wedding ceremony, the stage was by then cast in shadows. Only after a while does Puck, the Master of night–rule, return to the stage.

> Now the hungry lion roars
> And the wolf behowls the moon. . . .
> Now is the time of night
> That the graves, all gaping wide,
> Every one lets forth his sprite
> In the church–way paths to glide.
>
> (V.i.357–58, 365–68)

The somber line of Puck would be more appropriate for the night when Duncan was murdered than as a solemn "epithalamium" for the wedding night of the noble couple. The "screeching loud" (V.i.362) of the owl and "the triple Hecate's team" (370) are evoked in Puck's lines, as they were on the night of the regicide in *Macbeth*. It is the same night during which Romeo and Juliet, and Pyramus and Thisbe, committed suicide, during which Hermia might have killed Helena and Demetrius might have killed Lysander.

Hecate is *triformis:* Proserpina in Hades, Diana on earth, and Luna in the heavens. Hecate/Luna/Titania is the mistress of this midnight hour when night starts changing into a new day. But it is still the night during which elves dance "following darkness like a dream" (372). Wedding follows the evocation of the rite of mourning.

Puck is holding a broom in his hand; the broom was a traditional prop of the rural Robin Goodfellow: "I am sent with broom before / To sweep the dust behind the door" (V.i.375–76). In this sweeping of the floor there is a strange and piercing sadness. Puck sweeps away dust from the stage, as one sweeps a house. Sweeping away recurs in all carnival and spring rituals in England, France, Italy, Germany, and Poland. The symbolism of sweeping is rich and complex. A broom is a polysemic sign. But invariably sweeping away is a symbol of the end of the beginning of a new cycle. One sweeps rooms away after a death and before a wedding. Goethe beautifully shows this symbolism of sweeping on Saint John's Night:

> Let the children enjoy
> The fires of the night of Saint John,
> Every broom must be worn out,
> And children must be born.

In Eckermann's *Conversations with Goethe,* Goethe quotes his poem and comments: "It is enough for me to look out of the window to see, in the brooms which are used to sweep the streets and in the children running about in the streets, the symbols of life ever to be worn out and renewed."[46] Puck's sweeping of the stage with a broom is a sign of death and of a wedding which is a renewal. This is but the first epilogue of *A Midsummer Night's Dream.*

There is yet another. Oberon and Titania, with crowns of waxen tapers on their heads, enter the darkened stage with their train. They sing and dance a pavane. At a court wedding they might have invited the guests to participate in the dance together: "Every fairy take his gait" (402). Peter Brook, in his famous staging, had the house lights on while the actors stretched their hands out to the audience and threw them flowers.

Titania and Oberon appear for the second time in the play as the night doubles of their day shapes. If they are the same pair of actors who play Theseus and Hippolyta, Puck's soliloquy would give them enough time to change their costumes. The enveloping structure of the play has led, with astounding dramatic logic, to its final conclusion. Theseus and Titania, Philostrate, Hermia and Helena, Lysander and Demetrius—the spectators on stage of the "most lamentable comedy"—are the doubles of the audience watching *A Midsummer Night's Dream* in the house. The illusion of reality, as in Northrop Frye's succinct and brilliant formulation, becomes the reality of illusion. "Shadows"—doubles, are actors. But if actors—shadows are the doubles of spectators, the spectators are the doubles of actors.

> If we shadows have offended,
> Think but this, and all is mended,
> That you have but slumbr'd here,
> While these visions did appear.
>
> (V.i.409–12)

Only Puck is left on the stage. This is the third and last epilogue. "Gentles, do not reprehend" (V.i.415). As in *As You Like It* and *The Tempest,* the leading actor asks the public to applaud. But who is Puck in this third and last epilogue?

> The spirit Comus (Revelry), to whom men owe their revelling, is stationed at the doors of chamber. . . . Yet night is not represented as a person, but rather it is suggested by what is going on; and the splendid entrance indicated that is a wealthy pair just married who are lying on the couch. . . . And what else is there of the revel? Well, what but the revellers? Do you not hear the castanets and the flute's shrill note and the disorderly singing? The torches give a faint light, enough for the revellers to see what is close in front of them but not enough for us to see them. Peals of laughter arise, and women rush along with men, wearing men's sandals and garments girt in a strange fashion; for the revel permits women to masquerade as men, and men to "put on women's garb" and to ape the talk of women. Their crowns are no longer free but, crushed down to the head on account of the wild running of the dancers, they have lost their joyous look.[47]

This quote is from Philostratus, the Greek Sophist and erudite (ca. 176–245) whose *Imagines* became, during the Renaissance in Latin translation, one of the most popular textbooks and models for ancient icons of gods and mythical events. The most famous and most frequently quoted chapter of *Imagines* was "Comus." Shakespeare could not have found a more appropriate name for "Theseus' Master of the Revels." Philostratus became Philostrate at the "Athenian" court, so that in a system of successive exchanges he would be transformed into Puck, Lord of Misrule, and return in the epilogue to his antique prototype, the god of revelry and the festivities, Comus of the *Imagines* written by Philostratus the Sophist.[48]

There will always remain two interpretations of *A Midsummer Night's Dream:* the light one and the dark. And even as we chose the light one, let us not forget the dark one. Heraclitus wrote: "If it were not to

Dionysus that they performed the procession and sang the hymn to the pudenda, most shameful things would have been done. Hades and Dionysus are the same, to whichever they rave and revel.''[49] In the scene described by Philostratus, Comus is holding a torch downward. He is standing with his legs crossed, in a slumbering stance, at the entrance to the wedding chamber. His pose is that of a funerary Eros of Roman sarcophagi.[50] At the end of *A Midsummer Night's Dream*'s first epilogue, Puck could assume the pose of the funerary Eros. Shakespeare is a legatee of all myths.

But in both interpretations of *A Midsummer Night's Dream*, the bottom translation is most significant. Intellectual and dramatic richness of this most striking of Shakespeare's comedies consists in its evocation of the tradition of *serio ludere*. Only within this tradition of *"coincindentia oppositorum,"* of "the concord of this discord," does blind Cupid meet the golden ass and the spiritual transforms into the physical.

State University of New York at Stony Brook

NOTES

This essay was translated from the Polish by Daniela Miedzyrzecka, Columbia University.

1. All quotations from *A Midsummer Night's Dream* are taken from *The Arden Shakespeare,* ed. Harold F. Brooks (London: Methuen, 1979).

2. *The Praise of Folie,* ''A booke made in Latine by that great clerke Erasmus Roterodame. Englisshed by sir Thomas Chaloner knight. Anno 1549.'' All quotations after Clarence F. Miller edition (London: Oxford University Press, 1965).

3. Erwin Panofsky, ''Blind Cupid,'' in *Studies in Iconology: Humanistic Themes in the Art of the Renaissance* (1939; rpt. New York: Harper & Row, 1972, pp. 95–128; Edgar Wind, ''Orpheus in Praise of Blind Love,'' in *Pagan Mysteries in the Renaissance* (New York: Norton, 1968), pp. 53–80.

4. Frank Kermode, ''The Mature Comedies,'' *Early Shakespeare* (New York: St. Martin's, 1961), pp. 214–20; Paul A. Olson, ''*A Midsummer Night's Dream* and the Meaning of Court Marriage,'' *ELH* 24 (1957), pp. 95–119.

5. ''The commentary on a single text is not a contingent activity, assigned the reassuring alibi of the 'concrete': the single text is valid for all the texts of literature, not in that it represents them (abstracts and equalizes them), but in that literature itself is never anything but a single text: the one text is not an (inductive) access to a Model, but entrance into a network with a thousand entrances.'' Roland Barthes, *S/Z,* trans. Richard Miller (New York: Hill & Wang, 1974), p. 12.

6. *The Xi Bookes of The Golden Asse, Conteininge the Metamorphosie of Lucius Apuleius.* ''Translated out of Latine into Englishe by William Adlington. Anno 1566.'' Repr. 1571, 1582, 1596. All quotations after Ch. Whibley edition (London: 1893).

7. Mikhail Bakhtin, b. 1895, was connected in the early twenties with OPOJAZ (Society of Investigation of Poetic Language) and with the second phase of the Russian Formalist school. In the mid-thirties during the Stalinist purges, Bakhtin "disappeared," and some of his works were published under the names of his friends. He returned in the early sixties after nearly thirty years of literary "nonbeing." Two volumes have appeared in English: *Problems of Dostoevsky's Poetics,* first appeared in Russian in 1929 and a second, enlarged edition in 1963 (trans. R. W. Rotsel [Ann Arbor: Ardis, 1973]); *Rabelais and His World,* written in 1940, published in Russian 1965 (trans. Helene Iswolsky (Cambridge, Mass.: M. I. T. Press, 1968]).

8. Bakhtin, *Poetics,* pp. 88–89.

9. Claude Lévi-Strauss, *Le Cru et le Cuit* (Paris: Plon, 1964), p. 20.

10. Panofsky, "Blind Cupid," p. 137.

11. *The Basic Writings of Sigmund Freud* (New York: Random House, 1938), p. 572.

12. "Perhaps good king Oedipus had one eye too many." Hölderlin, *In Lovely Blueness.*

13. Wind, "Orpheus," p. 58.

14. Ibid., pp. 58–59.

15. Shakespeare's borrowings from *The Golden Ass* in *A Midsummer Night's Dream* (the meeting with the Corinthian lady, and the story of Psyche) were first noted by Sister M. Generosa in "Apuleius and *A Midsummer Night's Dream:* Analogue or Source. Which?" in *Studies in Philology* 42 (1945), pp. 198–204. James A. S. McPeek, "The Psyche Myth and *A Midsummer Night's Dream,*" *Shakespeare Quarterly* 23 (1972), pp. 69–79).

16. Emmanuel Cosquin, *Contes Populaires de Lorraine* (Paris: V. F. Vieweg, 1886), I, xxxii and II, 214–30.

17. Elizabeth Hazelton Haight, *Apuleius and His Influence* (New York: Cooper Square, 1963), pp. 90ff.

18. "The theme of role reversal was commonplace in folk imagery from the end of the Middle Ages through the first half of the nineteenth century: engravings or pamphlets show, for instance, a man straddling an upsidedown donkey and being beaten by his wife. In some pictures mice eat cats. A wolf watches over sheep; they devour him. Children spank parents. . . . Hens mount roosters; roosters lay eggs. The king goes on foot." Emmanuel Le Roy Ladurie, *Carnival in Romans,* trans. M. Finey (New York: Braziller, 1979), p. 191. "Hot ice" and "wondrous strange snow" (V.i.59) belong to this carnival language.

19. Passages from *Gargantua and Pantagruel* in Jacques Leclerq's translation (New York: The Heritage Press, 1964).

20. Claude Gaignebet, *Le Carnaval* (Paris: Payot, 1974), p. 120.

21. Rabelais possibly feared that the joke went too far, and this entire passage, beginning with "Does not Solomon" disappears in the second and subsequent editions of *Gargantua.* Rabelais also ironically quotes from Corinthians in chapter 8 of *Gargantua,* at the end of the description of his medallion with a picture of the hermaphrodite.

22. "Rabelais's entire approach, his *serio ludere,* the grotesque mask, is deeply justified by his conviction that true wisdom often disguises itself as foolishness. . . . Because he is the most foolish, Panurge receives the divine revelation; the 'Propos des bien yvres,' apparent gibberish, contains God's truth." Florence M. Weinberg, *The Wine and the Will: Rabelais's Bacchic Christianity* (Detroit: Wayne State University Press, 1972), p. 149.

23. Ronald F. Miller, in "*A Midsummer Night's Dream:* The Fairies, Bottom and the Mystery of Things," *Shakespeare Quarterly* 26 (1975), pointed out the possibility of a relation between Chaloner's translation and Bottom's monologue. This essay is perhaps the most advanced attempt at an allegorical, almost Neoplatonic interpretation of *A*

Midsummer Night's Dream; the "mystery of the fairies" points to "other mysteries in the world offstage" (p. 266).

24. Bakhtin, *Rabelais,* pp. 78, 199; Enid Welsford, *The Fool* (London: Faber and Faber, 1935), pp. 200ff; E. K. Chambers, *The Medieval Stage* (Oxford, England: Oxford University Press, 1903), I, chs. 13–15.

25. E. K. Chambers, *The Elizabethan Stage* (Oxford: Clarendon Press, I, pp. 158ff, 192. Henry appeared earlier in Daniel's masque *Twelve Goddesses* (1604), "taken out" and as a child "tost from hand to hand," I, 199.

26. Chambers, *The Elizabethan Stage,* I, 163–64: the reproduction of a painting on frontispiece in vol. I.

27. Letter of George Ferrars, appointed Lord of Misrule by Edward VI. Enid Welsford, *The Court Masque* (New York: Russell Russell, 1927), p. 146.

28. *A Midsummer Night's Dream,* ed. Henry Cuningham, Arden Shakespeare (London: Methuen, 1905), note to II.i.168. The poetic name of the love–potion flower was "lunary." In Lyly's *Sapho and Phao:* "an herbe called Lunary, that being bound to the pulses of the sick, causes nothinge but dreames of wedding and daunces" (III.iii.43); in *Endymion:* "On yonder banke neuer grove any thing but Lunary, and hereafter I neuer haue any bed but that banke" (II.iii.9–10). *The Complete Works of John Lyly,* ed. R. Warwick Bend (Oxford: Clarendon Press, 1902), III, 38 and 508.

29. The harmony of the string symbolizes for the Neoplatonists the *concordia discors* between the passions and the intellect: the bow's arrows wound, but the bow string itself is held immobile by the hand and guided by the controlling eye. Wind, "Orpheus," pp. 78f, 86f.

30. Ibid., p. 77.

31. In *The Arraignement of Paris,* performed at court ca. 1581–1584, published 1584, Venus bribes Paris; in this, "Venus' show," Helena appears accompanied by four Cupids. The court masque is mixed with pastoral play. Yet perhaps for the first time the "body" of a nymph who fell unhappily in love appears on stage with a "crooked churl" — a folk Fool. But even if Peele's play did not influence Shakespeare, it does nonetheless demonstrate how, at least ten years before *A Midsummer Night's Dream,* Neoplatonic similes of blind and seeing Cupid became a cliche of euphuistic poetry. ("And Cupid's bow is not alone in his triumph, but his rod. . . . His shafts keep heaven and earth in awe, and shape rewards for shame" [III.v.33,36]; "Alas, that ever Love was blind, to shoot so far amiss!" [III.v.7].) Only Shakespeare was able to put new life into these banalities.

32. The entertainment at Elvetham was prepared by, among others, Lyly, Thomas Morley, the organ player and choirmaster in St. Peter's, and the composers John Baldwin and Thomas Johnson. Ernest Brennecke, "The Entertainment at Elvetham, 1591," in *Music in English Renaissance Drama* (Lexington: University of Kentucky Press, 1968), pp. 32–172.

33. The *locus classicus* of Hermes, the *Psychopompos* who induces and dispels dreams, is in the first lines of the last book of the *Odyssey:* "Meanwhile Cyllenian Hermes was gathering in the souls of the Suitors, armed with the splendid golden wand that he can use at will to cast a spell on our eyes or wake us from the soundest sleep. He roused them up and marshalled them with this, and they obeyed his summons gibbering like bats that squeak and flutter in the depths of some mysterious cave" *(Odyssey,* trans. R. V. Rieu [Baltimore: Penguin Classics, 1946]).

34. "Fundamentally trickster tales represent the way a society defines the boundaries, states its rules and conventions (by showing what happens when the rules are broken), extracts order out of chaos, and reflects on the nature of its own identity, its differentia-

tion from the rest of the universe." Brian V. Street, "The Trickster Theme: Winnebago and Azanda," in *Zandae Themes,* ed. Andre Singer and Brian V. Street (Oxford: Oxford University Press, 1972), pp. 82–104. "Thus, like Ash-boy and Cinderella, the trickster is a mediator. Since his mediating function occupies a position half-way between two polar terms, he must retain something of that duality—namely an ambiguous and equivocal character." Claude Lévi-Strauss, *Structural Anthropology* (New York: Basic Books, 1963), p. 226.

35. During Elizabethan times Puck's part was always played by a mature actor, not by a young boy. In Restoration theater a ballerina would play the part of Puck, as well as Oberon. Peter Brook, in his *Midsummer Night's Dream,* repeated the Elizabethan tradition and had Puck's role performed by a tall and comical actor, John Kane ("thou lob of spirits," [II.i.16]).

36. "In the most solid and dramatic parts of his play (MND) Shakespeare is only giving an idealized version of courtly and country revels and of the people that played a part in them." Welsford, *The Court Masque,* p. 332. The most valid and complete interpretation of the festive world in Shakespeare's plays remains still, after over thirty years, C. L. Barber's *Shakespeare's Festive Comedy* (Cleveland: Meridian Books, 1959).

37. On the second day of uninterrupted spectacles Nereus appeared "so ugly as he ran toward his shelter that he 'affrighted a number of the country people, that they ran from him for feare, and thereby moved great laughter'" (Brennecke, "Entertainment," p. 45). Snout's fears that the ladies will be frightened by a lion are usually considered to be an allusion to the harnessing of a black moor to a chariot instead of a lion during the festivities of the christening of Prince Henry in 1594; perhaps it is also an amusing echo of "ugly" Nereus who frightened the ladies at Elvetham.

38. Even in Jonson, who introduced the "anti-Masque" or false-masque (in *The Masque of Blackness,* 1605), figures of the "anti-Masque" never mix with persons of the masque: they "vanish" after the "spectacle of strangenesse," before the allegories of order and harmony start.

39. For Shakespeare's use of terms "concord" and "discord" with musical connotations, see: *Richard II,* V.v.40ff; *Two Gentlemen of Verona,* I.ii.93ff; *Romeo and Juliet,* III.v.27; *The Rape of Lucrece,* 1124. See also, E. W. Naylor, *Shakespeare and Music* (New York: Da Capo Press B. Blom, 1965), p. 24.

40. Grimald's *Christus Redivivus,* performed in Oxford in 1540 (published in 1543) bears the subtitle "Comoedia Tragica." This is probably the earliest mixture in England of "comedy" and "tragedy" in one term. For the history of titles used by Peter Quince, it is interesting to note *The lamentable historye of the Pryunce Oedipus* (1563) and *The lamentable and true tragedie of M. Arden of Feversham in Kent* (1592). *The tragedy of Pyramus and Thisbe,* published by Geoffrey Bullogh *(Narrative and Dramatic Sources of Shakespeare* [London: 1966], III, 411–22) as an "Analogue" to *A Midsummer Night's Dream,* bears the subtitle: "Tragoedia miserrima." Chambers suspects that is a seventeenth-century product, perhaps by Nathaniel Richards. Bullough holds that it dates from the sixteenth century. Richards's authorship appears to me out of the question: the language and Latin marginalia suggest that this "Tragoedia miserrima" is earlier than *A Midsummer Night's Dream.*

41. Thomas Clayton, "'Fie What a Question That If Thou Wert Near a Lewd Interpreter': The Wall Scene in *A Midsummer Night's Dream,"* *Shakespeare Studies* 7 (1974), 101–12; J. W. Robinson, "Palpable Hot Ice: Dramatic Burlesque in *A Midsummer Night's Dream,"* *Studies in Philology* 61 (1964), 192–204.

42. The last words of Juliet ("O happy dagger, / This is thy sheath; there rest, and let me die") are not the most fortunate, and almost ask for burlesquing.

43. Three other interludes for wedding entertainments offered by Philostrate seem even less appropriate for the occasion. The strangest one is the first: "'The battle with the Centaurs, to be sung / By an Athenian eunuch to the harp'" (V.i.44–45). Commentators and notes invariably referred one to Ovid's *Metamorphosis* (XII. 210ff) or else to the "Life of Theseus" in North's *Plutarch*. But the *locus classicus* of this battle with centaurs in the Renaissance tradition was quite different. It is Lucian's *Symposium* or *A Feast of Lapithae*, in which the mythical battle of the Centaurs with the Lapitheans is a part of a satirical description of a brawl of philosophers at a contemporary wedding: "The bridegroom . . . was taken off with head in bandages—in the carriage in which he was to have taken his bride home." *The Works of Lucian of Samosata*, trans. H. W. Fowler and F. G. Fowler (Oxford: Oxford University Press, 1905), IV, 144.

In Apuleius' *The Golden Ass* unfortunate Charite also evokes the wedding interrupted by Centaurs in her story of her abduction by bandits from her would-be wedding: "In this sort was our marriage disturbed, like the marriage of Hypodame." Rabelais in *Gargantua and Pantagruel* also evokes that unfortunate wedding: "Do you call this a wedding? . . . Yes, by God, I call it the marriage described by Lucian in his *Symposium*. You remember: the philosopher of Samosata tells how the King of the Lapithae celebrated a marriage that ended in war between Lapithae and Centaurs" (bk. 4, ch. 15). Shakespeare's satirical intention in evoking this proverbially interrupted marriage appears self-evident.

44. Panofsky, "Blind Cupid," p. 140; and Kermode, *Shakespeare, Spenser, Donne* (London: Routledge Kegan Paul, 1971), p. 209: "To Pico, to Cornelius Agrippa, to Bruno, who distinguished nine kinds of fruitful love-blindness, this exaltation of the blindness of love was both Christian and Orphic."

45. Michel Foucault, in *The Order of Things* (1966; New York: Vintage Books, 1971), discusses in his chapter on *Don Quixote* this new confrontation of poetry and madness, beginning at the age of Baroque. But it is no longer the old Platonic theme of inspired madness. It is the mark of a new experience of language and things. At the fringes of a knowledge that separates beings, signs, and similitudes, and as though to limit its power, the madman fulfills the function of *homosemanticism:* he groups all signs together and leads them with a resemblance that never ceases to proliferate. The poet fulfills the opposite function: his is the *allegorical* role; beneath the language of signs and beneath the interplay of their precisely delineated distinctions, he strains his ears to catch that 'other language,' the language, without words or discourse, of resemblance" (pp. 49–50). But the poet in Theseus' lines is compared to the madman, and his function is to destroy the "allegorization." The exchange between the noble functions of mind and the low function of body is a radical criticism of all appearances, and an attempt to show a real similitude of "things" and "attitudes."

46. *Conversations with Goethe,* January 17, 1827. Quoted after Rabelais, pp. 250–51.

47. Philostratus, *Imagines,* trans. Arthur Fairbanks (London: W. Heinemann, 1931), pp. 9ff. Philostratus, a Greek writer (ca. 170–245), author of *The Life of Apollonius of Tyana* and of *Imagines,* was well known during the Renaissance. *Opera quae extant* in Greek with Latin translation had been published in Venice, 1501–1504, 1535, 1550, and in Florence in 1517. The "Stephani Nigri elegatissima" translation had at least three editions (Milan, 1521, 1532; Basel, 1532). *Imagines* was translated into French by de Vigenere; at least one edition (Paris, 1578) dates from before *A Midsummer Night's Dream* (Paris, 1614; L'Angelier Repr., New York; Garland, 1976). *Imagines* was extensively commented upon and quoted by Gyraldus and Cartari, whose *Le imagini dei degli antichi* often reads like a transcript of Philostratus.

Imagines was highly esteemed by Shakespeare's fellow dramatists. Jonson directly quoted Philostratus six times in his abundant notes to his masques (i.e., in a note to "Cupids" in *The Masque of Beauty*, 1608: "especially *Phil.* in Icon. Amor. whom I haue particularly followed in this description" *Works,* Hereford and Simpson, ed. [Oxford: Oxford University Press, 1941], VII, 188). See Allan H. Gilbert, *The Symbolic Persons in the Masques of Ben Jonson,* (Durham: Duke University Press, 1948), pp. 262–63. Samuel Daniels referred to *Imagines* and followed very precisely its image of Sleep in *The Vision of Twelve Goddesses* (1604): "And therefore was Sleep / as he is described by Philostratus in *Amphiarai imagine* / apparelled." *A Book of Masques* (Cambridge: Cambridge University Press, 1967), p. 28.

48. For over a hundred years commentaries suggested the source of the name Philostrate is borrowed from Chaucer's *The Knight's Tale.* But Chaucer's lover, who goes to Athens under the name of Philostrate, and Shakespeare's master of the revels have nothing in common. The author of *Imagines* as a possible source for the name of Philostrate is a guess one is tempted to make. Philostratus' Comus is generally thought to be the main source for the image of Comus opening Jonson's *Pleasure Reconcild to Vertue* (1618) and for Milton's *Comus* (1634). *A Midsummer Night's Dream* and the two plays have of ten been compared: Jonson's *Pleasure* with *Comus* (Paul Reyher, *Les Masques anglaises* [Paris, 1909; New York: B. Blom, 1964], pp. 212–13; Welsford, *The Court Masque,* pp. 314–20; the editors of Jonson, *Works,* II, 304–09); *A Midsummer Night's Dream* with *Comus* (Welsford, *The Court Masque,* pp. 330–35, Glynne Wickham, *Shakespeare's Dramatic Heritage* [London: Routledge & Kegan Paul, 1969], pp. 181–84). But the real link between these three plays is the image of Comus in *Imagines* (1.2). See also Stephen Orgel, *The Jonsonian Masque,* (Cambridge, Mass.: Harvard University Press, 1965), pp. 151–69. Orgel compares the passage on Comus from Philostratus with Cartari's *Le imagini* and describes the iconographic tradition stemming from *Imagines.*

49. Fragment B 15. Quoted from Albert Cook, "Heraclitus and the Conditions of Utterance," *Arion,* n. s. 2/4 (1976), p. 473.

50. Wind, "Orpheus," pp. 104, 158.